I didn't even know there were eldercare attorneys before reading this book. Within months I was consulting one myself on behalf of my own father. **Navigating the Eldercare Journey** *is an indispensable guidebook for this complex and emotionally charged journey we Boomers must make with our parents. Jodi Clock skillfully weaves together a life story that helps explain the many challenges we face with medical, financial, and other elder life planning issues. Issues most of us should confront sooner, rather than later.*

Having worked closely with funeral service professionals for years, I'm convinced that Jodi Clock's book belongs in the resource center of every funeral home in America. Her narrative walks the reader through a story so many of us face firsthand in our own families. As we confront the myriad of issues and emotions caring for aging parents, it's important to understand that your hometown funeral director can be an invaluable resource in reducing stress by helping solve many of these challenges of elder care.

Mark Jorgensen
President, Global Recruiters of Batesville

* * *

Your guidance throughout the past months was a sensational blessing to my family and most importantly my mother, from her care, wishes, and final resting place.

There are many events that are a part of our journey in life, some joyous, sad, expected, or unexpected. My mom always said she did not want to be a burden in her later years. She met with her attorney 20 years ago, preplanned her funeral, executed a Living Trust and a DNR and had it all packaged in a "special envelope." When she was diagnosed with early Dementia we were heart broken and unaware what lied ahead. We quickly realized we needed to find a quality place for her to live and properly care for her, review her health coverage and finances. Not knowing her time left with us, it was difficult to make decisions without emotion. Your book gave us guidance and comfort when interviewing the assisted living residence, trying to understand Medicare and Medicare programs, and making sure we had the appropriate documents to properly manage her finances and most importantly her wishes. As we opened the "special envelope," we realized we did not have all the documents we needed, including the Financial POA and the Medical POA. We found a wonderful place for her to live as she quickly progressed through the stages of Alzheimer's in a matter of months. We are at peace knowing she was in the best place of care, her finances were accessible for her needs, her medical coverage was complete which gave her the best possible health care, and her wishes were complete as she was laid to rest where she belonged in her beloved Michigan. Jodi's guidance and experience gave my mom what she deserved, the very best, just as she was...

Lori Palmer

* * *

It seemed as if one day my mother was driving and participating in daily activities at her senior living apartment and then next we were faced with needing to move her to a nursing facility. Then all of the questions were coming in faster than we had answers....

Who do you turn to for answers? The facilities and Medicare are not consistent with their answers; somebody tells you one thing today and their answer is different tomorrow, and many of the websites are frauds when it comes to senior care. Thank God we know Jodi Clock! Jodi took the time to outline important things that we had to do: powers of attorney for medical and financial, home health care, occupational therapy, and more.

Once we had received the word that mom passed away, Jodi was there to help. She contacted the funeral home in Michigan to ensure that all the necessary items were being handled correctly, and when she discovered that the casket that was provided was not up to her standards, she went out and found one of better quality, picked it up, and delivered it to the funeral home. During the funeral Jodi was there not only as a friend supporting the family, but also I noticed her coordinating all of the activities to ensure that everything went smoothly and that nothing was missed. As the casket was being lowered, she asked them to stop so she could pull ⋯ to have as a memory of my mother. Jodi made a painful day very special.

Chris Liebum

Navigating the Eldercare Journey

...Without Going Broke!

by Jodi M. Clock

Navigating the Eldercare Journey... Without Going Broke!

Windy City Publishers
2118 Plum Grove Rd., #349
Rolling Meadows, IL 60008
www.windycitypublishers.com

Published in the United States of America

10 9 8 7 6 5 4 3 2 1

First Edition: 2012

Library of Congress Control Number: 2011942839

ISBN: 978-1-935766-27-8

Cover Design and Production by Amanda Inkinen

Windy City Publishers

Chicago

To Marie Perkins and Janet Switzer

INTRODUCTION

This easy-to-understand guide takes you from the basics of qualifying for Medicaid to planning a funeral—and covers why these things are important. Your parents can legally keep their hard-earned cash—and so can you. I'll show you how, based on 22 years of experience helping regular families just like yours.

I wrote this book in response to the questions my husband and I answer every day in our funeral home. So many people come in seeking advice on end-of-life issues when it's too late. Had they begun their journey earlier with a seasoned eldercare expert, they would not only already have a solution, they would be able to leave something behind for their children and grandchildren. End-of-life planning can mean the difference between leaving a legacy and dying penniless.

You have a choice. If you elect not to proactively safeguard both your and your parents' monetary assets—leaving them exposed and unnecessarily taxed when death occurs—expect to be emotionally drained and physically paralyzed by not knowing what "to-do" item to do first! The advantage of handling these affairs ahead of time is that it enables you to focus on what's important at this particular moment in time; therefore enabling you to prepare a plan to follow for the future. Each situation is different in terms of prioritization, so don't beat yourself up on "would of, could of, and should of"—just address the situation at hand and move forward. No matter how prepared you think you are, the reality of death is sobering. When time is on your side, you can make well-thought-out decisions.

TABLE OF CONTENTS

CHAPTER 1:
THE NEED FOR END-OF-LIFE FINANCIAL PLANNING

In this chapter you will learn:

1. The five stages of the healthcare spin cycle
2. How to pay for healthcare
3. The difference between Medicaid and Medicare
4. How to make some tough decisions

RUSS AND YVONNE

Yvonne's Secret

"And what will you have, Sir?" asked the waitress who had just taken Yvonne's order.

"I'll have what she's having! After being married for twenty-five years, we may not look alike, but we like the same things," said Russ with a big smile.

"Great!" the waitress replied as she walked away to place their dinner order. She couldn't help but giggle at the cute and happy couple.

This year marked a special point in Russ and Yvonne's marriage. They had both been married before. Russ's marriage had ended in divorce, and Yvonne had been a widow when they met. But they had now been married to each other longer than they had been to their first spouses.

Russ picked up his cocktail glass for a toast. "To you, Kid!"

Toasting each other was a daily ritual. Yvonne clinked her glass to his, grateful that neither Russ nor anyone else knew what she was thinking. She wondered how long she could continue this charade. In the past year Russ's ability to read had been declining. This started to become apparent to Yvonne when Russ stopped ordering off the menu. Instead, he would playfully ask Yvonne, "Kid, what sounds good tonight?" Regardless of her response, he'd smile and say she was a mind reader. "I'm a lucky man!" he'd often say.

Yvonne tried to keep up appearances so that Russ wasn't placed on the spot. She didn't want to inadvertently put him in a situation that could expose his memory loss and cause him embarrassment. The effort was becoming stressful. She knew it was beginning to take a toll on her, both mentally and physically. Still, Yvonne wasn't ready to discuss the matter with their blended family of adult children. She hoped that it would be a while before any of them caught on. She just wasn't ready to talk about it, even though she knew she would have all the support she needed. Somehow, she was overcome with the feeling that she'd be betraying a trust. Russ and Yvonne were a team; they had been each other's rock since the day they said "I do." *In time things will take care of themselves*, she thought. *Things always do*. Russ had always taken care of Yvonne; it felt only natural that she do the same.

Yvonne first noticed that Russ's memory and independence were fading about two years before. It had happened so gradually and subtly that compensating for it had just become part of life for her. The things Russ forgot weren't major; in fact, she often had similar memory lapses herself—misplacing the checkbook or car keys, getting frustrated with the TV remote, and forgetting where she had parked the car. Nothing to get excited about—until Russ began to repeatedly ask questions about things he should have known, and no longer took an interest in things they had been doing together for years, like playing cribbage and double solitaire. When he lost interest even in golf, Yvonne realized that something was seriously wrong, and she could not fix it for him.

As these changes in Russ's memory started to become obvious to her, Yvonne began to take notes. She recorded the day, date, and time she observed a new behavior pattern. She also started gently asking or telling Russ what to do around the house rather than waiting for him to take the initiative. Yvonne also knew that she had to take inventory of their affairs. She needed to make sure all their legal documents were current. When she and Russ had married 25 years ago, they had drafted their last will and testament and even a durable power of attorney, but they had not made any amendments since then. It wasn't that they hadn't thought of it—they had even discussed it—but somehow other things just took precedence.

Yvonne had the wisdom to know that if she didn't take action now, things wouldn't get done the way she and Russ had envisioned. They both had adult children from their first marriages. It wasn't that their children wouldn't or couldn't handle matters; it was just that Yvonne did not want to place this burden on them. She and Russ were very private about their financial affairs, and Yvonne did not want to make their affairs public in the probate court system. She had witnessed that when her mother had died. She also had experienced what can take place between siblings, even close siblings on the best of terms, when sentimental items and money are involved. She was determined to save their family from unnecessary headaches.

From the beginning Russ and Yvonne were careful to blend their families. When they made the decision to marry, the children they brought into the marriage—along with the responsibility that went with them—were just part of the deal. There was no "his" or "hers;" it was a mutual feeling of "ours." This was important then and still was now. Their grandchildren knew Russ and Yvonne only as their grandparents; not as "step" grandparents.

As Yvonne started to review their affairs, she promised herself that there would be a clear direction for their children to follow.

* * *

"The question is not whether we will die,
but how we will live."

–Joan Borysenko

It's not a secret that we all have a 100-percent probability of aging, regardless of how much we try to fight it. We can diet, exercise, or even have plastic surgery—but in the end, the results are the same. We will age, and our parents will age. Aging often goes hand-in-hand with mental and physical deterioration, which may limit the ability to live independently. Facing this situation in our parents' lives forces us to make hard decisions.

We can be proactive about end-of-life plans while our parents still have health, wealth, and mental clarity, or we can put off these plans and be forced to make major decisions in moments of crisis.

More often than not, people take the latter path and see their parents' life savings, 401(k)s, IRAs, life insurance, and entire assets whittled away. Instead of leaving an inheritance for their family, people can see their entire net worth—which took them a lifetime to accumulate—devoured by long-term care expenses, probate costs, income taxes, and estate taxes.

Having "The Talk"

How do you have "the talk" with your parents about wills, finances, medical care choices, and funerals? Elderly parents may be reluctant to face end-of-life issues. This may be due to one of three reasons: procrastination; lack of experience or information; or denial.

If you are thinking about asking your parents about planning their end-of-life affairs, you are most likely motivated by love and concern. You are hoping to:

- Honor their wishes regarding personal items, medical decisions, and funeral preferences.
- Avoid making hasty and emotional decisions in a crisis.
- Prevent overspending due to not knowing your parent's wishes.

Sadly, elderly parents sometimes misconstrue their children's concern as nosiness. Even worse, they may see it as an attempt to take over management of their personal affairs. Many of today's seniors were raised not to discuss these issues openly, so don't be surprised if the first response you hear is, "None of your business." At some point, no matter how awkward this conversation may feel as an adult child, if your parents have not initiated this dialog, you will have too.

Key Point

Just because people are aging or beginning to face health challenges doesn't mean that they are insensitive, ignorant, or incapable of decision-making.

HISTORICAL PERSPECTIVE

Our parents were brought up in times when the "real world" was often their only formal education. Manufacturing jobs were plentiful and they learned from their parents that a strong work ethic was the key to success. Our parents understood how to budget, save, and raise a family on one income, so that children could have a parent at home.

Up until the late 1970s or so, there wasn't a great need for eldercare decisions. Families weren't so fragmented by divorce or geography. If an elder needed care, the family figured out a way to handle it. On the infrequent occasion a person did require care in a nursing home, the stay wasn't for an extended period of time. Not too many years ago, people entered a nursing home when death was near because in-home hospice care was very not as popular as it is today.

Our parents aren't oblivious to the fact that they are aging. It is simply that medical and health advances, coupled with the vast cultural changes that have occurred in their lifetime, have created age-related issues that previous generations never had to face.

ONE WAY ➡

Moody's most recent report states that a woman who is 50 can expect to live an average of another 31.6 years, and a man the same age can expect to live another 28.8 years.

For more information on life expectancy, go to http://www.efmoody.com/estate/lifeexpectancy.html

MARKER MOMENTS

It is human nature to disregard or avoid difficult issues. On some level, our parents know that they need to discuss end-of-life issues. It's not unusual for elders to avoid these issues until a "marker moment" occurs. Even then, it can be uncomfortable.

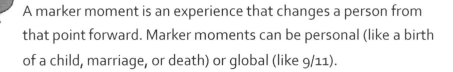

KEY POINT

A marker moment is an experience that changes a person from that point forward. Marker moments can be personal (like a birth of a child, marriage, or death) or global (like 9/11).

Statistics indicate that about 70 percent of today's elderly have in some manner raised end-of-life issues with at least one of their adult children. If there is more than one adult child in the family, the geographically closest one often ends up taking over the caretaking responsibilities and legal and financial matters, by default making some very difficult decisions. Usually, the closest female adult child becomes the go-to person.

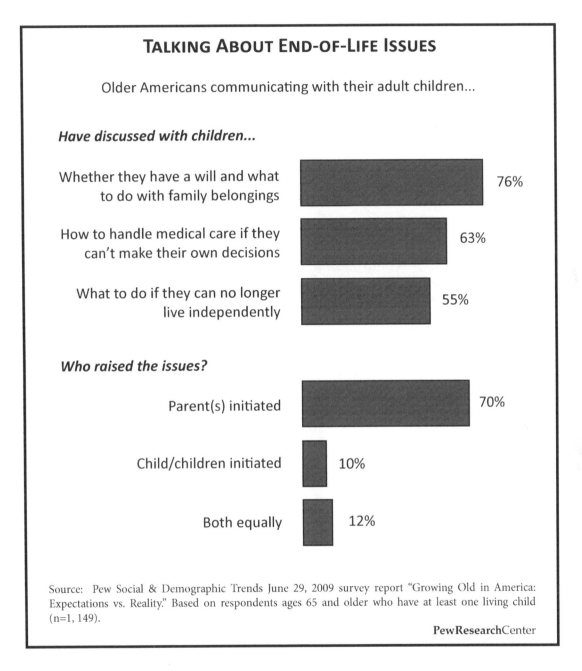

TALKING ABOUT END-OF-LIFE ISSUES

Older Americans communicating with their adult children...

Have discussed with children...

Whether they have a will and what to do with family belongings — 76%

How to handle medical care if they can't make their own decisions — 63%

What to do if they can no longer live independently — 55%

Who raised the issues?

Parent(s) initiated — 70%

Child/children initiated — 10%

Both equally — 12%

Source: Pew Social & Demographic Trends June 29, 2009 survey report "Growing Old in America: Expectations vs. Reality." Based on respondents ages 65 and older who have at least one living child (n=1, 149).

PewResearchCenter

What about the remaining 30 percent who don't address this subject with their adult children? Unless someone has had to make medical or funeral decisions or has experienced probate court on behalf of someone else, he or she is unlikely to be proactive in these matters.

How to Have "The Talk" with Your Parents

Setting the Stage

If you are not willing to wait for a "marker moment" to have this type of conversation with your parents, try to engage them.

That doesn't mean that saying over coffee, "Could you please pass me the creamer, and oh, by the way, have you thought about what will happen if one of you gets sick and has to go into a nursing home or dies?" Nor does it mean grilling your parents with questions and putting them on the spot.

Engaging them means using leading questions to guide the conversation gently toward this topic in a non-confrontational manner. Your questions should be thought-provoking and should pave the way for future conversations.

Possible Leading Questions

One idea is to introduce the topic by placing the focus on yourself. Share with your parents that you were thinking about your own mortality and estate-planning issues and ask them for some advice.

- Do they have any medical advance directives?
- How they feel about the refusal of life support?
- Do they have a living will?
- Do they have a durable power of attorney in place?
- Do they have a list of all the medications they are on?
- Do they prefer a local hospital, or would they prefer to travel to a specific one?

This is an excellent place to start since the focus is not on their "things" or their money. It also will give you insight into how organized they are.

Getting a person to discuss his living wishes is much easier than entering into a discussion about his death. This breaks the ice for future conversations and forces your parent to realize that others need to be aware of his wishes. He is more likely to be more forthcoming if you approach it from the standpoint of wanting to be helpful in a crisis.

Your lead-in question could be something like, "Dad, have you ever thought about what will happen if Mom outlives you?" Once you have asked that, be quiet! Even if it's a long few moments of silence, let your parent process the question. The less you say, the more you will learn.

Observe your parent's body language. If his arms are folded and he looks surprised or defensive, it's clear that you have caught him completely off guard. Proceed with caution!

Once you've gotten the dialog going, you can transition to questions like:

- "Have you taken care of your estate?"
- "Do you have a will?" If the response is yes, ask them where it is and what to do if something should happen to them both simultaneously.

Keep the conversation going by asking all kinds of "what if" questions.

MEETING RESISTANCE

If your parents are not willing to discuss things with you now, let them know that you would appreciate some direction in the near future.

Emphasize that your interest is based not on greed, but on concern and love. Convey to them that you'll be happy to table the conversation and let the two of them discuss it between themselves, but that you will ask them again. After all, it's only fair that you shouldn't have to have a discussion of this magnitude in a hospital emergency room.

If your parents haven't made plans of this nature, let them know it's okay and that you'll be happy to help them through the process by giving them the names of some eldercare and estate planning experts for them to call. It's not uncommon for your local funeral home, senior resource groups and community centers to have a list of solid referral sources.

If they are concerned about expenses, reassure them that it may not be as costly as they think and that many times there is no charge for consultations. Let them know that the financial and emotional costs of doing nothing are far greater. Remind them that if nothing is protected, the only winner is probate court. (Chapter 7 focuses on this in detail.)

THE HEALTHCARE SPIN CYCLE

Psychologists have identified five distinct phases of life:

1. Childhood
2. Adolescence
3. Young adulthood
4. Middle age
5. Old adulthood

Many people refer to the fifth stage of life as the "golden years." Professionals who work in senior healthcare and legal affairs refer to this last stage of life as a time when people require "eldercare."

Still others who deal with end-of-life issues have identified a pattern that occurs when a senior's health begins to deteriorate: the "healthcare spin cycle." This is a sequence of health-related events during the end-of-life phase. It is not necessarily age-driven.

Life isn't a straight line; the stages of the healthcare spin cycle do not necessarily follow each other in this order. These are probabilities based on established patterns, not certainties, but the end-of-life healthcare spin cycle looks something like this:

1. Alive and well
2. Injury or illness
3. Hospital stay or in-home care
4. Assisted living or nursing home
5. Hospice and death

KEY POINT

The key is to recognize when your loved one has entered phase 2 of this cycle, to acknowledge it and know exactly where he is, and then to make financial changes to position him properly.

This pattern often repeats many times, depending on the person's health issues, and all too often becomes an emotional and financial black hole. The financial consequences of this cycle can be devastating for the average person, but they don't have to be. With the proper guidance, a solid strategy can minimize and even stop financial devastation. What you can do depends on where a person is in this cycle.

If a person is 65 today, it's likely that he will live well into his 80s.

KEY POINT

Not everyone experiences the healthcare spin cycle in order. It's not uncommon for people, once they become ill, to move between stages 2 and 4 for months, if not years. It's also not uncommon for a senior in a nursing home facility to have multiple ailments.

Families who have proactively positioned their loved one's affairs and assets often report that when the end stages of life arrive, they are better able to focus on what is really important and not stress over a daunting "to-do" list, especially in stages 4 (assisted living or a nursing home) and 5 (hospice/death).

Chances are high that your parents or loved ones will receive Medicaid assistance in the end. Your parent's assets could end up unnecessarily depleted, while you become mentally drained, seeking out countless "self proclaimed" experts who are in good faith providing you with pieces and parts of information, only to discover in the end are obsolete or, worse yet, exasperate your individual situation. This doesn't have to happen if you are financially proactive. The key to guarding your loved one's nest egg is knowing the financial allowance guidelines for Medicaid, which differ depending on the marital status of the person in need of care. Regardless of marital status, it's always easier—and certainly less expensive—to position assets now rather than during a crisis.

SEEING A LIFE SAVINGS DWINDLE AWAY

What happens when you can no longer take care of your loved one and you are faced with placing him into a nursing home or care facility? What happens if your children face this same situation when trying to care for you?

Your loved ones are at risk of losing everything they have worked their entire lives for. This is no exaggeration; this is a reality. People who enter long-term care facilities will most likely deplete their life savings in less than one year, often in fewer than 120 days.

What happens when your loved one runs out of money to pay for care?

- He or she may have to sell personal effects.
- His or her nest egg will be depleted.
- There will be no inheritance for the family.

Eventually your loved one will become financially dependent on government assistance (Medicaid). Medicaid is a United States government program providing hospitalization and medical insurance for people of all ages within certain income limits. For more information, visit Centers of Medicare and Medicaid services at: http://www.cms.gov.

KEY POINT

For the purposes of this book, a "crisis" is when a person has exhausted his Medicare benefit and is attempting to qualify for Medicaid assistance to pay for care in a nursing home or skilled-care facility.

 End-of-life financial planning is not the same as financial planning. There are strict, clear federal and state rules to follow. If you know what you are doing, you can maximize the financial benefits allowed by these rules.

PAYING FOR HEALTHCARE

Paying for healthcare in today's world is a real issue—combining the need for in-home assistance or nursing home care to the mix just adds fuel to the fire. If these real-life story problems are not addressed situationally, they could be explosive. The healthcare spin cycle idea isn't revolutionary; most of us have observed this cycle, whether or not we knew how to label it. Be aware of these stages to establish financial planning goals to include end-of-life healthcare for your parents. By the time the last phase arrives, there should be no surprises and little left to question.

So what are your payment options for end-of-life care? Personal insurance will be in effect during the first three stages of the healthcare spin cycle (alive and well, illness or injury, and hospitalization). It is the fourth phase of the cycle—assisted living or nursing-home care—that will require financial planning to cover the costs that exceed any primary medical insurance or Medicare benefits. I briefly examine the three payment options available below. Chapters 2 and 3 delve more deeply into long-term care, Medicaid, and other issues that you'll need to clearly understand as a caregiver or decision-maker.

Payment options for the fourth phase of the healthcare spin cycle are:

- Medicare: 20-100 days
- Long-term care (LTC) insurance
- Private pay (using life savings)
- Medicaid (if eligibility requirements are met)

There are advantages and disadvantages to each choice. The payment option you select will be determined by your family's value set.

Payment Options for Assisted-Living Care

Option 1—Medicare

"Medicare is a national health insurance program created and administered by the federal government in the U.S. to address the medical needs of older American citizens. Medicare is available to U.S. citizens 65 and older and some people with disabilities under age 65," according to the Encyclopedia of Surgery (http://www.surgeryencyclopedia.com/La-Pa/Medicare.html#ixzz1ABWbvGLM).

Using Medicare for long-term care isn't an option. Medicare is designed to pay for up to only 20-100 days of care. It is an option for short-term skilled care.

Option 2—Long-Term Care Insurance

Determining whether or not your parent can use long-term care insurance is straightforward. When your parents reach stage 4 of the healthcare spin cycle, rather than ask, "Can my parents purchase long-term care insurance?" instead ask, "Did they purchase this form of coverage?" If the answer is "yes," investigate to determine the care options covered under the policy. If this form of protection was not purchased, then you must explore other options, as your parent will most likely not qualify for this type of coverage, and if they do, the premiums would be outrageous. In this case you are better off to seek out alternative methods for payment.

Option 3—Private Pay

Many people mistakenly think that if nursing-home care is necessary, their privately purchased Medicare supplement insurance or their long-term care policy and Medicare will pay for their stay. This is only partly true. If you or your parents decide to pay for nursing home care privately (with your own funds), these are some things you and they should know:

- All private Medicare supplement insurance and/or long-term care insurance policy deductibles must be met. Once the deductibles have been satisfied, that policy will begin to pay for a specific number of days in care, depending on the type of private-pay insurance policy. Many policies clearly state a maximum number of days for which payment will be made.

- After the first 20 days of care covered by Medicare have passed, expect to be presented with an invoice beginning on the 21st day unless your loved one has a Medicare supplemental policy or a long-term care policy. The invoice will account for all care arrangements, including food and medications.
- The average monthly expense of nursing-home care is around $6,500.
- The average stay is three years.

Will you or your loved one have this amount of money to pay for care?

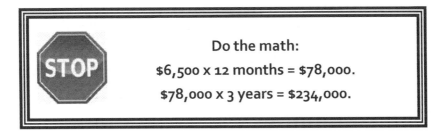

Do the math:
$6,500 x 12 months = $78,000.
$78,000 x 3 years = $234,000.

Questions to ask yourself prior to using the private-pay option
- Is there a spouse or dependent/disabled child who will need to maintain his or her standard of living? How many months of care can be covered before the money runs out?
- What will the source of these funds be? Options include:
  - ○ Checking accounts
  - ○ Savings accounts
  - ○ Annuities
  - ○ Stocks/Bonds/Mutual funds
  - ○ Retirement funds/Pensions
  - ○ Cash surrender value of life insurance policy
- What happens if the spouse or dependent/disabled child becomes ill? Will private pay still be feasible?
- In the end, would you or your loved one end up having to qualify for Medicaid *and* end up broke?

OPTION 4—MEDICAID

Medicaid is a viable payment option for everyone over age 65 and those who are blind or disabled in need of care when entering or residing in a nursing home. If a person satisfies any or all of the parameters just listed and is single, the qualification process for Medicaid is very straightforward. They can move forward to the next step required by their state. If this person is married, there are different measures to take depending on their situation, which will be addressed later.

Ultimately the litmus test looks like this:

- ✓ Age 65 or older
- ✓ Blind or disabled
- ✓ In need of medical care or assistance

If the above qualifications are met, is this person:

- A married person in need of care with a living spouse who does not need care?
- A married couple in need of care?
- A single person in need of care?

THE EMERGENCE OF MEDICAID PLANNING

Receiving Medicaid assistance to pay for end-of-life care is based primarily on net worth and income of the person in need of care. This person's financial assets cannot exceed a certain amount. If they do, he will be required to pay for care privately until his assets are depleted to the point at which he qualifies. This often means that people enter a "spend down" cycle that depletes their nest egg. With good planning, however, you can properly position and reallocate your parents' assets to preserve their nest egg and also allow them to qualify for Medicaid.

Up until the last 20 years or so, it was not necessary to reposition assets into a living trust to qualify for Medicaid assistance. Why? The average life expectancy was not as long as it is today. In our parents' generation, living to age 80 was equivalent to living to be 90 or even 100 years old today.

IMPORTANT POINTS ABOUT MEDICAID

- You can complete the qualification paperwork yourself or seek the assistance of an eldercare attorney.
- You can obtain Medicaid applications from your county's Human Services Department, from an eldercare attorney, or from the nursing home where care is being sought or given.
- Social workers often aid with the application or the approval process.
    - Each state has different requirements for qualification.
    - The federal "look-back" period is five years for all gift-giving or transfers. If money was transferred or "gifted" during the past five years, there will be a penalty.
    - Documented proof (for a given period of time) of monthly bills, bank statements, insurance contracts, and veteran paperwork are just some of the items necessary to qualify.

KEY POINT

If the end result is going to be the same—needing to qualify for Medicaid—why not begin with the end in mind?

If the result will ultimately be having to qualify for Medicaid in order to pay for care, why not qualify to begin with, enabling the person in need of care the ability to leave behind some financial assets for a family member, friend, or even charity?

WHERE TO GO FOR HELP

Some potential sources of information about qualifying for Medicaid include:

- Friends and family who have been through a similar experience
- Social workers and community help centers
- Eldercare attorneys

Friends and Family

KEY POINT

People usually first turn to friends and family for information. This is natural. It's easy. It's comfortable. It is also <u>wrong!</u>

While friends and family who offer you advice no doubt mean well, it is very difficult to know all the rules and variables of the Medicaid program. Laws differ by state and by marital status, and they change all the time. The guidelines followed six months ago by your cousin who lives two states away were likely entirely different from the guidelines that you must follow today. Seek emotional comfort and guidance from your friends and family. Seek financial guidance from professionals.

Social Workers and Community Volunteer Service Centers

It's not uncommon to be assigned a social worker to help you with the Medicaid application process. Although this help can be welcome, keep in mind three important things:

1. Not all social service caseworkers understand how to navigate within the guidelines of Medicaid rules. Caseworkers can be misinformed about qualification and make recommendations that aren't in their clients' best interests. The laws change so frequently that often caseworkers are the last to know. The same is true for community volunteers offering free assistance.

2. Caseworkers have stressful jobs, earn minimal pay, and often have unmanageable workloads.

3. Social service caseworkers are government employees. It is not their job to show people how to reallocate their assets in a way that still allows them to qualify for Medicaid.

 A caseworker may tell you that asset reallocation is impossible and that it borders on Medicaid fraud. This is not true! You will not be hiding any assets if you fully disclose everything you do to reposition wealth you or your parents have.

Everything done to protect one's assets is fully disclosed, accounted for, and revealed within the Medicaid documents that must be completed by, or on the behalf of the applicant and turned into the case worker as a component of the approval qualification process. Neither this book nor any reputable eldercare attorney will ever suggest anything illegal. This book simply reveals legal methods to help you navigate within the system.

Eldercare Attorneys

An eldercare attorney? Yes! Many attorneys specialize. If you were having brain surgery, you would hire a neurosurgeon, not a general practitioner. So when you are seeking Medicaid application assistance, find an attorney who specializes in eldercare.

To find an eldercare attorney with solid references, ask around. Contact professionals who regularly interact with this type of specialist. Your local funeral director, funeral home preplanning specialist, private cemetery salesperson, financial planner, guardian agency, or anyone who has placed a parent or grandparent in a nursing home has probably dealt with attorneys who excel in this area. The more people you ask for recommendations, the more likely you are to hear the same name multiple times. Check this person out. Google him or her. Call the Better Business Bureau and the Chamber of Commerce. Determine their history and credibility. Don't fall for a yellow-page ad or hire the first name you hear.

A good eldercare attorney will custom design an asset protection plan, provide you with a price for that plan, and tell you what assets will be able to be preserved. If your attorney can't confidently provide a solution, a timeline, and an end result you can live with, run! This attorney is not a specialist in this field.

Hiring an attorney may initially seem expensive, but the question to ask yourself is, "Compared to what?" The money you spend on a good attorney will likely more than pay for itself in the assets he or she will help you protect.

How to Find an Expert Eldercare Attorney

Look for someone who will ensure that your loved one will be able to:

- Qualify for Medicaid to pay the entire cost of a long-term stay in a nursing home while preserving assets for those left behind.
- Legally hire an individual (possibly a family member) to provide personal care at home and secure funding for the care.
- If necessary, financially provide for a disabled child or grandchild without creating a Medicaid penalty.
- Preserve his or her assets and qualify for 24-hour skilled nursing care.

ONE WAY →

If the eldercare attorney you consult says:

- "Come back after you have spent down the applicant's funds."
- "You can have only one prepaid irrevocable funeral."
- "Cash out your life insurance policies to pay for care."
- "Sell your second car."
- "Sell your home (or your second home)."
- "It's too late to protect anything."

… get a new lawyer!

The attorney should be able to help you save money even if your loved one is already in a nursing home. He or she should also be able to discuss issues regarding rental property and preserving income. Ask him or her how life insurance policies with cash value can work for your parents with minimal tax consequences.

Don't take chances. Your family attorney may be a great person and even a friend, but if you don't like what you hear, get a second or even a third opinion. It's no different from seeking medical care: You are in control!

Making Tough Decisions

Other Important End-of-Life Decisions

Once you have made financial arrangements for end-of-life care, you will face many other decisions concerning this final stage of life. If you are in a position to talk with your loved one about these matters, creating a road map for these choices can help your family cope with very difficult issues.

Take Care of the Paperwork

The documents listed below enable others to act on behalf of a person receiving care if he has become unable to speak for himself. They help ensure that the person's wishes are respected.

- Durable Power of Attorney (DPOA) for financial decisions
- DPOA for medical decisions
- Health Care Advance Directives/Living Will
- Do Not Resuscitate (DNR) Orders
- Organ/Tissue donation choices

Other highly recommended legal documents:

- Living Trust
- Last Will and Testament

"...through the use of comprehensive advance directives there is an opportunity for sizable savings, particularly if [money is] being spent on procedures and treatments that do not comply with patient wishes."

—Fay A. Rozovsky

Discuss these documents and decisions with your loved ones and make sure you know their wishes. Chapters 5, 6, and 7 focus on these documents.

ONE WAY →

Did you know that even the terminally ill typically do not have DNR orders in place? A *New York Times* article by Paula Span suggested that the term DNR, an acronym for "Do Not Resuscitate," may sound too harsh to some people. She suggested a change from DNR to AND: "Allow Natural Death." Don't get hung up on the terms or acronyms; instead, focus on what's important—providing the proper documents so the voice of the person in care will be heard.

FUNERAL DECISIONS

While it may seem macabre to discuss a person's funeral before he or she is dead, this is an important part of end-of-life planning. The decisions a person makes should be documented with their funeral home.

If the loved one in your care is in the fourth stage of the healthcare spin cycle (assisted living or nursing home care), and he or she plans to use Medicaid, you will be encouraged—if not required—to prepay for his or her funeral prior to Medicaid qualification. This can protect assets, as Chapter 3 covers. At a minimum, a funeral plan (discussed in the Appendix) should include:

- Disposition preference (burial or cremation)
- Religious or memorial service preferences
- Biographical information for a death certificate and obituary

To get the most out of the information in this chapter and to avoid having to make difficult decisions during a crisis, help your loved one complete the "End-of-Life Care Needs: Letter to Family" on the following pages and keep it in a secure place.

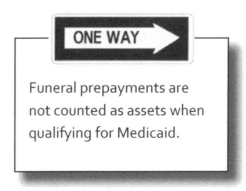

ONE WAY

Funeral prepayments are not counted as assets when qualifying for Medicaid.

FAMILY CARE PLAN

End-of-Life Care Needs:
Letter to Family

Date: _____

Dear _____ (Name of caregiver/spouse/other),

I have made some decisions regarding my healthcare financing. These decisions are above and beyond medical insurance and Medicare and go into effect when my health deteriorates to the point that I am unable to take care of myself.

If I should go into a nursing home, my care will be paid by:

_____   My long-term care insurance.

_____   My personal savings until all funds have been used; then Medicaid.

_____   Medicaid: I have proactively repositioned my assets so that I should qualify after my insurance and Medicare will no longer pay.

_____   I have not proactively repositioned my assets, but want to have my assets repositioned so that Medicaid will pay for my care.

The attorney I have been working with is: _____

Telephone: _____ Email: _____

Address: _____

FAMILY CARE PLAN

I have or have not completed the following paperwork (circle one):

Have	Have not	Durable Power of Attorney (DPOA) for finances
Have	Have not	DPOA for health care
Have	Have not	Health Care Directives/Living Will
Have	Have not	Do Not Resuscitate (DNR) orders
Have	Have not	Organ/Tissue donation choices
Have	Have not	Living Trust
Have	Have not	Will
Have	Have not	Funeral plans

Important documents or information to help you complete the above forms can be found at this location:

_____

Respectfully and with love,

Signature

(Name)
(Address)
(City, State, Zip)

Witness: _____

Date: _____

CHAPTER 2:

UNDERSTANDING COVERAGE OPTIONS

In this chapter you will learn:
1. Healthcare financing alternatives
2. The basics of the Family and Medical Leave Act (FMLA) and the Consolidated Omnibus Budget Reconciliation Act (COBRA)
3. What long-term care (LTC) insurance is and what to look for in a policy
4. More intricacies of Medicare and Medicaid

RUSS AND YVONNE
Preparing for Changes

Russ, a retired sales representative, enjoyed traveling, playing cards, golfing, and bowling with Yvonne and their friends. After Russ's retirement, they became spontaneous. It wasn't uncommon for them to pack a bag or two, toss their golf clubs in the car, and see where the road less traveled took them.

Russ loved driving. Together he and Yvonne would seek out golf courses they hadn't played, play nine holes, and then find a delightful place to unwind for the evening.

This changed last summer when Yvonne noticed Russ was becoming slightly confused when driving, especially at night. She knew his memory was slipping and had been for quite some time, but she still felt safe with Russ driving while she sat in the passenger seat. His reflexes were still sharp, and his driving ability was not impaired. But he would forget a few turns here or there, so she would remind him where to turn or act as a copilot and navigator. This became comfortable. When Russ got tired or didn't feel like driving, Yvonne would take the wheel.

Until a few years before, Russ and Yvonne's medical bills had been pretty typical, with some not-uncommon medical procedures. There were regular stress tests to monitor Russ's heart because he had undergone bypass surgery in his early fifties. But since then, he hadn't had any difficulties. Beyond that, there had been a few aches and pains that ended up being arthritis, some age-based tests such as colonoscopies, and a cataract surgery.

Russ had taken an early retirement, and the package provided him and Yvonne with privately paid health care that Medicare did not cover. They had only to cover their annual deductible and prescription co-payments. The company even had a reimbursement plan for employees and retirees to use toward dental and vision coverage.

Russ and Yvonne considered themselves incredibly fortunate, since many of their friends had to pay much of this personally and then rely on Medicare; some were even on Medicaid.

Long before retirement, they had purchased long-term care insurance. Yvonne was insistent on this for two reasons. Both she and Russ did not ever want to be a burden to their adult children, some of whom had families of their own.

Yvonne never voiced the second reason. For many years Yvonne had secretly carried guilt about not caring for her mother. Grandma Ruby, as she was affectionately called, had suffered with Parkinson's disease for almost half of her adult life. Grandma Ruby had lived to be 83. During the final five years of her life, she had been unable to live alone, and in her last year she had required around-the-clock care.

Grandma Ruby lived out of state and was incredibly stubborn and unwilling to move. Fortunately, Aunt Carol, Grandma Ruby's younger sister, was also a widow and lived in the same town. Aunt Carol was 12 years younger than Grandma Ruby and full of energy; she selflessly took it upon herself to care for her sister. After a while she moved out of her apartment and into Grandma Ruby's house to provide around-the-clock care.

Words could not express the gratitude Yvonne and her siblings felt for Aunt Carol. Her help allowed them to live their lives without disruption. Each of them loved their mother, but none was in a position to move in with her. Grandma Ruby didn't care about who took care of her, but she wanted to stay in her home.

Aunt Carol went to a seminar and learned valuable information she could use as a caregiver. The seminar was held by an eldercare attorney who helped families in times of medical and financial crises. This attorney's forte was teaching people how they could qualify to have Medicaid pay for long-term care and not go broke in the process. Aunt Carol liked what she heard and even met with this attorney. As a result she was able to:

- Let Grandma Ruby remain in her own home and become her full-time caregiver
- Move into Grandma Ruby's home and get paid to take care of her
- Receive caregiver support and respite when needed
- Prepay for Grandma Ruby's funeral and guarantee the price
- Retain ownership of the home for Grandma Ruby's heirs after her death instead of having to sell it to repay Medicaid
- Continue to live in Grandma Ruby's home
- Avoid probate costs on the home
- Pass a small financial legacy to Grandma Ruby's children

Grandma Ruby had died nearly 10 years ago, but Yvonne remembered it as if it were yesterday. She was so grateful that her mother had preplanned and paid for her funeral because there had then been no questions about what she wanted. With Aunt Carol's help, Grandma Ruby's children knew that their mother was well taken care of, that her finances were safe, and that her funeral was exactly the way she wanted it. This had a huge impact on Yvonne.

* * *

"It's no longer a question of staying healthy.
It's a question of finding a sickness you like."
–Jackie Mason

Born between 1946 and 1964, the generation of Americans affectionately known as the "Baby Boomers" is about to make its next great cultural contribution. In 2011, the first Baby Boomer turned 65, and over the next decade a flood of people will begin participating in Medicare and Medicaid programs. This generation will have a dramatic impact on our country's perceptions of aging, caregiving, illness, and end-of-life options.

 To get the person in need the high-quality healthcare he or she deserves, you need to know what insurance the person has. Insurance coverage helps determine healthcare options.

UNDERSTAND YOUR ALTERNATIVES

How successfully you navigate among your loved one's healthcare options—and how well you preserve his or her wealth—will depend on how well you understand and use public and private programs.

Consider these facts from an article by Theresa Tamkins that appeared on CNN.com in 2009:

- 62.1 percent of bankruptcies in America in 2009 were medically related.
- Many people had more than $5,000 (or 10 percent of their pretax income) in medical bills and chose to mortgage their homes to pay them.
- Job loss can be a byproduct of a serious illness. This loss of income combined with mortgages and illness-related debts can become too much to handle.

- On average, medically bankrupt families had $17,943 in out-of-pocket expenses: $26,971 for those who lacked insurance and $17,749 for those who had been covered by insurance at some point.
- On average, 78 percent of those who went bankrupt had health insurance, but were bankrupted anyway because of gaps in coverage such as co-payments, deductibles and uncovered services.

KEY POINT

A caregiver must:
1. Know what types of financial assistance programs exist
2. Understand the intricacies of those programs
3. Know what insurance his or her loved one already has

What Is My Role?

Helping Family (Finding Benefits for the Caregiver)

When we receive bad or even tragic news about our health, we first turn to our family and friends. If we are lucky, we will have family—children, siblings, or other close relatives—who will be willing to help. But at some point in your life, you may find yourself caring for an elderly parent or spouse, in-law, or relative.

You may find that caring for your loved one drains your time and energy. You may need to apply for Family and Medical Leave Act (FMLA) benefits. The FMLA was implemented during the Clinton Administration to provide some relief to families dealing with loved ones in chronic ill health or long-term care.

KEY POINT

FMLA enables eligible employees to obtain up to a 12-week leave from work per fiscal year (not calendar year) so that they can provide care for a family member. For more information, visit the Department of Labor website at www.dol.gov.

Although the time off is guaranteed by FMLA, compensation is not. You are allowed 12 weeks of leave without pay. However, if you receive health benefits as part of your job, the benefits must, by law, remain in force during this period.

Depending on your financial situation, using the time you are allowed through FMLA may be enough to see your family through its crisis. For many people in these situations, however, living without a paycheck for three months just isn't feasible.

Other factors may prevent you from providing in-home care to your loved one, such as:

- The absence of a personal support system
- Inability of other family members to help you care for your loved one
- Your own poor physical heath
- Geographic distance from the loved one
- Lack of funds
- Lack of necessary medical skills

You may find yourself pressured into the caregiver role. You may feel cultural expectations, pressure from family members, an honest desire to help, and guilt or resentment. But even if you cannot provide in-home care to a loved one, you can still act as a caregiver.

KEY POINT

Many laws (such as privacy laws and the Health Insurance Portability and Accountability Act of 1996 [HIPAA]) are cumbersome and a nuisance; however, they must be taken seriously, and employers must abide by them. Administrators are not trying to be difficult; they are just trying to remain in compliance while they assist you.

Researching Private Healthcare Benefits

If your loved one is unclear about the type of healthcare coverage they have, or unable to provide you with the written plan coverage information about his or her health insurance, you will need to locate it or call the provider in question to determine what, if any, private healthcare benefits he or she already has.

If the person in your care is under the age of 65, he or she may be covered by a private healthcare plan. This plan may a company health plan, a spouse's health plan, or an individual health plan purchased through an insurance agent.

Don't assume that someone who is unemployed does not have insurance. Many people pay independently for their insurance, either through personal plans or previous employers in accordance with the Consolidated Omnibus Budget Reconciliation Act (COBRA). Enacted by Congress in 1986, COBRA requires qualified employers to continue to offer group insurance plans to terminated employees (and even survivors of employees when death occurs while employed) for a limited time.

COBRA is used as a form of "gap" insurance until a person becomes covered under a new employer's health plan or gains coverage through governmental healthcare plans such as Medicare or Medicaid. COBRA will allow an individual to participate for up to 18 months.

See http://www.dol.gov/dol/topic/health-plans/cobra.htm.

The benefit details of private healthcare providers and plans are too numerous to list here. To research your loved one's health insurance, start at the source. Call the previous employer's human resource department, or the insurance carrier itself, and request an explanation of benefits. This will save you valuable time and answer many of your questions.

"PACE" It Out

The Program of All-Inclusive Care for the Elderly (PACE) is founded on the belief that seniors are better cared for by their families or communities than by institutions.

PACE is modeled after eastern Philippine and Asian communities, where families do whatever they can to take care of their elderly. This practice was first replicated in American Chinatowns and has spread through the country. In order to receive PACE benefits individuals must be:

- At least 55
- Diagnosed as chronically ill
- Certified by a physician or the state as needing nursing-home care

PACE offers:

- Delivery of medical supplies
- Supportive care services
- Adult day care that offers nursing; physical, occupational, and recreational therapies; meals; nutritional counseling; social work; and personal care
- Medical care by a PACE physician familiar with the history, needs, and preferences of the participant
- Home health care and personal care
- Prescription drugs
- Social services
- Medical specialists such as audiologists, dentists, optometrists, podiatrists, and speech therapists
- Respite care
- Hospital and nursing home care when necessary

PACE is funded by both Medicare and Medicaid. In some cases the enrollee is required to pay a monthly fee. Sadly, PACE is available in only 27 states at the time this book was published.

Long-Term Care Insurance

Long-term care (LTC) insurance policies have become increasingly popular over the last 25 years. In fact, LTC coverage has turned into a niche insurance business.

LTC insurance is specifically designed to cover custodial care expenses for an extended period of time. Care can be provided in a person's home, an assisted living facility, or a nursing home, depending on the type of coverage. "Custodial care" includes assisting with activities such as bathing, dressing, eating, bathroom needs, and taking medications.

Custodial expenses can also include adult day care, caregiver respite, meal delivery, visiting nurses, shopping or chore services, and possibly other qualifying programs of this nature.

Aside from the obvious benefits of LTC insurance for the beneficiary, a secondary benefit is that it eases some emotional and financial burdens for caregivers.

If you wait too long to purchase it, LTC insurance becomes prohibitively expensive. It becomes very pricey after age 55. The ideal age range for purchasing LTC insurance is the mid-to-late 40s to early 50s.

> **ONE WAY →**
>
> States that participate in PACE: California, Colorado, Florida, Hawaii, Illinois, Iowa, Kansas, Louisiana, Maryland, Massachusetts, Michigan, Missouri, Montana, New Jersey, New Mexico, New York, North Carolina, North Dakota, Ohio
>
> For more information about PACE, see www.npaonline.org/website/article.asp?id=65

KEY POINT

Long-term care insurance is specifically designed to cover custodial care.

WHAT TO LOOK FOR IN LONG-TERM CARE INSURANCE

Know your policy! Some companies will pay for only one type of care, while others will pay for several types. Types include:

- Home health care
- Adult day care
- Assisted living care
- Nursing home care
- Hospice care

While it may be too late to purchase LTC insurance for your loved one, it may still be an option for your own future care. Make sure you are investing your money with a company that is reputable and has a solid A.M. Best rating. (A.M. Best is a rating company that assesses insurance companies' financial strength.)

Premium prices can vary greatly and are driven by coverage type and waiting period. The more services you require, the more your premium will cost. The more limited your policy is, the lower the premium. Read the fine print so there are no surprises or misunderstandings when it's time to use your policy.

Daily benefit is also a key consideration. This is the amount per day that your policy will pay toward long-term care. Anything that isn't covered by the LTC insurance policy is the insured's responsibility. The amount of daily benefit will depend on your premium. The length of time the daily benefit will be paid is called the *benefit period*.

ONE WAY →

Many people assume that Medicare and private pay will cover the first 100 days of care. Don't assume—read your policy. Medicare will cover the first 20 days. Any more time must be requested and approved.

The *waiting period* is the amount of time before your policy becomes active. This can range from 0 to 120 days. The waiting period you select will depend on how much you are comfortable paying for out of your own pocket.

Take into consideration other means of payment, such as personal savings, private health insurance, and Medicare. Remember, the shorter the waiting period, the higher the policy premium.

KEY POINT

There may be a gap between when Medicare stops paying and when your Medicare supplemental policy or LTC insurance policy kicks in. You will be expected to pay for care privately during the interim.

People purchase insurance and riders to cover their cars, homes, dental care, vision care—and even their vacations on the off-chance a trip will be canceled! As we continue to live longer, the chances that we will need some type of long-term care increase. LTC insurance assures us that we will be cared for without suffering financial hardship. It empowers us to decide where we will be cared for and by whom.

Understanding Medicare and Medicaid

Regardless of what private healthcare we held while employed and what LTC insurance policy we may have purchased, most of us will eventually use Medicare and possibly Medicaid. The transition from private healthcare to government healthcare may be intimidating.

Many so-called professionals profess to be experts on Medicare and Medicaid—but beware. Many of these sources are for-profit organizations that have a vested interest in selling products or services to complement government programs.

You may find it necessary to purchase services to augment your coverage. But before you do, make sure you understand what the government healthcare programs are and how they work.

WHAT'S THE DIFFERENCE?

Medicare and Medicaid are two completely separate government healthcare programs with specific guidelines and purposes.

Both Medicare and Medicaid are "entitlement programs" that are available to U.S. citizens who meet certain criteria. Beyond this, they are two entirely different programs that have two entirely different purposes. All too often people confuse them.

Medicare

Medicare is a healthcare program available to U.S. citizens who:

- Are 65 or older
- Have worked since they came of age (18 and older)
- Have paid into the Social Security system their entire careers (regardless of gaps in employment; the requirement is based on the number of quarters a person has worked since the age of 18)
- Have paid federal income taxes

Those who don't satisfy these government requirements can purchase Medicare Part A during specified enrollment periods.

Medicare also offers private-pay insurance to complement or fill in the "gaps" in the program. Medicare rules allow private carriers to use the Medicare name when selling supplemental insurance, which can be confusing.

Medicaid

Medicaid is a government healthcare program designed to assist people with low income and certain population groups (deaf or blind people, uninsured pregnant women, uninsured children 19 and younger, the aged, and the disabled) with doctor visits, prescription drugs, emergency room visits, hospital stays, and even nursing-home care. Medicaid provides assistance for the "medically needy" who could not otherwise afford medical care. Eligibility is based on income and assets. Assets include houses, cars, checking accounts, investments, and savings accounts.

Each state manages its own Medicaid program and establishes its own eligibility requirements. To find out about your state's requirements, visit https://www.cms.gov/home/medicaid.asp.

Medicaid has a broad range of coverage. In this book, "Medicaid coverage" refers to nursing-home care for the "aged" as defined by the U.S. Department of Human Services. See https://www.cms.gov.

KEY POINT

Here's a trick for remembering which program is which:

- Medicare is for people 65 and older because when people reach retirement age, the government cares about their health.
- Medicaid provides aid for those who are in need of health services but can't afford them.

How Do Medicare and Medicaid Work Together?

Medicare provides proactive medical care for senior citizens and includes coverage for short hospital stays. Medicaid "takes over" where Medicare leaves off (stops paying for coverage) and addresses nursing-home care or long-term care. The following chart shows what each program covers.

An overview of coverage provided by Medicare and Medicaid

	Medicare	Medicaid
Public health program	Yes	Yes
Helps pay medical bills	Yes	Yes
Insurance company involved	Yes	No
Based on financial need	No	Yes
Has age restrictions/requirements	Yes	Yes
Based on medical need	No	Yes
Charges deductibles and co-payments	Yes	Yes
Federal program	Yes	Yes
State partnership	No	Yes
Varies by state	No	Yes
State managed/directed	No	Yes
Requires that assets are exhausted or turned over to the state	No	Yes

You may be wondering why, if Medicare is for the aged and Medicaid is for the financially needy, it is important to understand both programs. The answer is that it will save you time, energy, and money on the eldercare journey. Many aged persons in long-term care must navigate between these two different programs. While documentation must

If you are a U.S. citizen and meet the qualifications, you are entitled to use these government healthcare programs.

show that your loved one is financially needy and requires long-term medical care, there are legal ways to preserve some of his assets and still apply for low-income-based care.

Key Point

All too often people assume that skilled or nursing-home care is 100 percent covered by Medicare. In fact, deductibles and criteria must be met.

ONE WAY

2010 Medicare Coverage for Long-Term Care

Number of Days	You Pay	Medicare Pays
1-20	Nothing	Everything
21-100	$137.50 per day	The balance
Over 100	Everything	Nothing

KEY POINT

Medicare will not pay for care after the 100-day mark!

After the 100th day, a person in long-term care has three options:

- Leave the facility and seek care from a private venue (friends or family).
- Pay privately. (Average monthly rates are $6,000-plus.)
- Seek residency at a facility that accepts Medicaid (upon qualification, the government will pay 100 percent of daily expenses in a facility that accepts Medicaid).

ONE WAY

A government program called Supplemental Security Income (SSI) assists people who are low-income, 65 or older, blind, or disabled. Do not confuse SSI with Medicare or Medicaid. It is beyond the scope of this book.

If you would like to learn more about this program visit www.socialsecurity.gov or call 1-800-772-1213.

Understanding Medicare and Medicare Supplements

Find out how many days-in-care your private medical insurance policy will cover before Medicare requires joint pay participation. This is subject to change, so be sure to monitor it yearly.

There are four sections of Medicare coverage. Medicare Parts A and B are government programs for those who qualify. Parts C and D are private supplements to the government program and must be purchased. Let's look at each of these in detail.

Medicare does not cover all medical expenses; it covers only pieces and parts!

Medicare Part A

This is the original plan the government introduced to help pay for hospital bills and that taxpayers pay for through payroll deductions. Medicare Part A is premium-free and covers:

- Inpatient hospital care
- Inpatient stays
- Inpatient rehabilitation
- Long-term hospital care
- Skilled nursing facilities
- Home health care
- Hospice

Part A has deductibles, preset co-payments, and sometimes even participating or accepted physician networks.

Medicare Part B

Part B is an insurance option to supplement Part A. Think of Part A as "hospital insurance" and Part B as "medical insurance." Part B pays for outpatient and physician services as well as some preventive services.

Covered services include items such as:

- Physical or occupational therapy
- Ambulance services
- Bone-density tests
- Clinical lab services
- Flu shots
- Certain diabetic supplies

Participants must pay a premium for Part B as well as pay coinsurance and deductibles. If someone fails to sign up for Part B when he or she is first eligible, the premium will increase by a certain percent for each 12-month period that he or she could have been enrolled but was not. An exception to this is if the participant was covered by an employer's group health plan during that period.

Medicare Part C

This is an optional private-pay program that individuals can purchase privately and that behaves like a Health Maintenance Organization (HMO) or a Preferred Provider Organization (PPO). It's often referred to as a Medicare Advantage Plan and includes both hospital and medical insurance (i.e., original Medicare parts A and B). In order to join a Medicare Advantage Plan, your loved one must be enrolled in Medicare parts A and B and live in a service area covered by the plan. These plans are offered by private insurance companies that are Medicare-approved. Medicare pays a certain monthly amount to these plans for the participant's care. Those who opt to enroll in a Medicare Advantage Plan are still responsible for the monthly premium for Medicare Part B. There are co-payments for most of the services covered by these Part C plans, and some plans have annual deductibles.

Medicare Part D

Part D is another optional private-pay program that helps cover the cost of prescription drugs and may be purchased by those participating in Medicare. Medicare drug plans are offered by private insurance companies that are approved by Medicare. The plans have different costs, and some drugs may be covered by one plan but not another, so investigate a number of plans before choosing one. Even if an eligible person is not currently taking any prescription medications, enrolling in Part D may still be a good choice since there may be a penalty for late enrollment.

Medigap

Medigap is yet another optional private-pay program designed to cover the "gaps" not covered in the Medicare parts A and B. It pays coinsurance, co-payments and deductibles under Medicare parts A and B only.

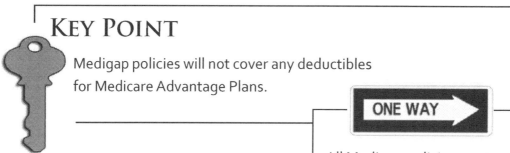

KEY POINT

Medigap policies will not cover any deductibles for Medicare Advantage Plans.

ONE WAY

To keep things simple, think of Medicare (parts A and B) as an insurance program that contributes to the payment of primary care. *Primary care* means doctor appointments and necessary, brief hospital stays.

All Medigap policies must clearly be labeled "Medicare Supplement Policies" and be clearly identified with the letters A–N on the card. Medigap policies must follow federal and state laws and are standardized regardless which insurance company sells them to you.

KEY POINT

Parts C and D are <u>not</u> government-paid programs; they are optional.

Medicare parts A and B are available to any individual or couple who contributed to the Medicare program during their working years. Part A focuses on the hospital-stay portion of the system, while part B pays for a portion of doctor visits that are outpatient services.

Parts C and D are private-pay programs that are meant to augment or offset other medical costs. Both are non-governmental programs sold by private insurers. These may be good fits for many individuals; it would be wise to check into them as the potential liability of incurred unexpected expenses can dramatically impact one's financial situation. Assess the existing and potential medical needs and compare coverage to any retirement health benefits that are already in force. Keep in mind that any individual's medical needs will most likely increase with age.

Consumers must pay privately for Medicare Parts C and D.

Healthcare Coverage Options Checklist

1. LTC Insurance Checklist

_____ Determine whether the person in need of care owns LTC insurance. If he or she does, read the policy, including the fine print, or consult the agent in order to understand what type of coverage is provided.

If the person in need of care is healthy and has no LTC insurance, is repositioning assets, and is in his or her 50s, price out the coverage to decide if it's worth purchasing.

If the person in need of care has no LTC insurance and has liquid assets, he may want to self-fund his care. Ask a trusted financial advisor about the best way to do this.

Use this LTC financial calculator to determine how much money to set aside based on your loved one's age and gender. Or use it as a guide to determine how much LTC insurance to purchase.

http://www.longtermcare.gov/LTC/Main_Site/
Planning_LTC/Considerations/Savings_Calculator.aspx?rand=5

2. Medicare Checklist

_____ If the person in need of care is not receiving Social Security and will soon be 65, make sure he or she is signed up to receive monthly Social Security benefits three months before turning 65, ensuring no delay in benefits. Visit the Social Security website (www.socialsecurity.gov) or call 1-800-772-1213 or 1-800-325-0778 (deaf or hearing impaired).

_____If the person in need of care is 65 and not on Medicare, it's time to sign him or her up for plans A and B.

_____Study the costs and benefits associated with Medicare Part C and Part D and decide if these additional plans will benefit your loved one.

3. Medicaid Checklist

If the person in need of care will participate in Medicaid to finance long-term care, his assets will need to be reviewed and possibly repositioned. He will need to qualify for coverage based upon the guidelines of the state in which he lives.

_____ Become familiar with the county website to learn about specific Medicaid rules and requirements, read frequently asked questions, and download applications or forms.

_____ Visit the county Department of Human Services and obtain a Medicaid qualification application from a caseworker. (If the person in care is already in a nursing home, the nursing home's caseworker can give you this.)

_____ Find a reputable eldercare attorney to assist you if the person in care has significant assets, multiple cars, homes, boats, or RVs, or the process may become too overwhelming.

CHAPTER 3:

MYTHS AND FACTS ABOUT MEDICAID

In this chapter you will learn:
1.   How to qualify your loved one for Medicaid
2.   How to choose the right attorney

RUSS AND YVONNE

Getting the Paperwork in Order

Yvonne kept all their important papers in the top drawer of the filing cabinet in Russ's office. Russ liked to have a place where he could sit and read the newspaper, review their stocks, and listen to the news. It was also the area of the house designated for trophies, awards, and memorabilia from Russ's career. Yvonne even had a few golf and bowling trophies of her own on display.

While Russ was taking a nap, Yvonne went into the office, looked through the filing cabinet, and began writing down exactly what they had. The good news was that she and Russ had a designated area for important paperwork. The bad news was that no one knew exactly what was in those drawers. It had been years since either of them had taken the time to go through them. As Yvonne began her scavenger hunt, the first file she came across was labeled "Insurance." She opened it and found all kinds of things, including receipts, policies, handbooks, and notes, and soon realized that this file was in no particular order. As she leafed through it, she found life insurance documents, health insurance guidelines, pharmaceutical mail-in forms, their home policy, her jewelry riders, automobile coverage, and their long-term care policy. It took Yvonne about an hour to sort through it all, but when she was done, she had made new folders for each insurance category. Now the information was accessible and current.

At the front of each folder she recorded some relevant information:

- Name of the insurance company
- Type of insurance by category: life, auto, home, health, long-term care
- Coverage amount
- Deductibles, if any
- Names of the life insurance beneficiaries
- Any outstanding loan against any of the policies

Yvonne also discovered two insurance policies she had no idea they had. The policies had been issued to them free of charge through their credit union. There was a term life policy for $7,000 on each of them that was paid in full as long as they remained members. This was a pleasant surprise.

By the time Yvonne was finished, she heard Russ out in the kitchen trying to stir up something to eat after his nap. She figured she had done enough for one day and would begin again fresh tomorrow.

If your loved one is seeking long-term, end-of-life healthcare and financially qualifies for the program, Medicaid will pay for the entire cost of a long-term stay in a nursing home. Let's discuss how to do that without becoming financially destitute.

* * *

The following is a list of the most commonly heard fears, concerns, and untruths about Medicaid. Those who impart these myths either don't understand how to navigate within the system or are misinformed. Let's dispel them once and for all.

Medicaid Myths

Myth 1: My parents have Medicare, so they won't need Medicaid.

As we learned earlier (in Chapter 2), Medicare is *not* Medicaid. Medicare is a government health program that acts as major medical insurance for U.S. citizens who are age 65 or older. (Some disabled people meet the criteria and qualify at a younger age.) Medicare covers hospital expenses for those who qualify, and additional, optional Medicare programs will cover doctor's visits and prescription drugs. Medicare will cover only the first 20 to 100 days of extended care before private-pay, long-term care insurance, or Medicaid must take over.

Myth 2: The person in need of care has long-term care insurance, therefore Medicaid isn't needed.

Great! Long-term care insurance is a wonderful purchase. Depending on the type of coverage purchased, however, it may or may not cover nursing-home care. It's critical that you read the fine print and determine what it will and will not pay for.

Key Point

One out of nine U.S. citizens is over the age of 65. This is an estimated 38.9 million people. Of those 38.9 million people, approximately 1.3 million are receiving care in a nursing-home facility and this number is growing daily. Within the remaining non-institutionalized segment of those individuals age 65 and over, 24 percent are in poor health and living at home and 6.4 percent are currently receiving some form of care within the home. These statistics will only dramatically increase as time goes on. (From the Centers for Disease Control and Prevention: www.cdc.org.)

Myth 3: I can take care of my loved one in need of care.

It may be unrealistic to assume this responsibility. Most families today no longer live in close proximity to one another. It's not uncommon for adult children to live several hours away, or even in a different state—or country—from their parents or relatives. It's always safest to plan for the worst and hope for the best. If you can physically and financially assume responsibility for your parents' or loved one's long-term care, they are very fortunate. But as their health declines, they may need more than you can give.

Myth 4: A person must "go broke" before he or she can apply for Medicaid and qualify to stay in a nursing home.

This is probably one of the biggest myths. Those who "go broke" by spending down their assets to apply for Medicaid do so based on misinformation. What they do not realize is that an expert eldercare attorney or an estate-planning attorney could have reallocated their assets and legally navigated within the system to preserve a financial legacy for their spouse, children, grandchildren, or favorite charities, while still enabling them to qualify for Medicaid benefits for nursing-home care.

Myth 5: The government took my parents' or loved one's house when they went into the nursing home.

The government doesn't take away people's houses. The family did not title the house properly, which left it exposed and available for the government to use to recoup its Medicaid financial outlay.

MEDICAID—JUST THE FACTS

Here are the straightforward requirements for qualifying for Medicaid assistance. To be eligible for Medicaid you must be:

- A U.S. citizen
- Disabled *or* age 65 and older
- Able to meet an income "means" test
- Considered medically needy and in need of assistance

Under the current rules, most middle-class seniors don't automatically qualify for Medicaid. In most states, people must "spend down" their assets until they are considered poor, or "financially needy," to be eligible for Medicaid. There are, however, legal ways to reposition assets to qualify for Medicaid while preserving some financial assets for loved ones. People don't have to become destitute or broke.

Medicaid considers the assets and income of both spouses when one or the other seeks nursing-home benefit payments.

Countable assets include:

- Cash, savings, and checking accounts
- Real estate (other than the primary residence)
- More than one vehicle
- Boats
- Recreational vehicles
- Stocks
- Bonds
- Mutual funds
- Credit union share and draft accounts
- Certificates of deposit
- U.S. savings bonds

- Pension plans
- Individual retirement accounts (IRAs)
- Keogh plans
- Nursing-home trust funds, prepaid funeral contracts that can be canceled, trusts (depending on the terms)
- Tax-deferred annuities
- Promissory notes
- Cash value of life insurance
- Securities
- Uncashed checks

Non-countable assets include:
- Primary residence
- One car/vehicle titled asset
- Household effects
- Personal jewelry and clothing
- Prepaid funeral or burial account
- Value of life insurance if face value or cash is $1,500 or less
- Term life insurance policy

KEY POINT

Other kinds of assets may be either countable or non-countable, depending upon how your state has categorized them. Your state Medicaid office can provide the exact lists it uses to categorize assets.

Qualifying as a Community Spouse

When a married person enters a long-term care facility, the spouse who is not entering the nursing home is referred to as a "community spouse." Some rules regarding the amount that the community spouse is allowed to keep are below:

- The community spouse can keep all of his or her own income and half of all joint income, up to a maximum amount established each year. (Maximum amount determined by state government.) This may be referred to as a "spousal income allowance." This is above and beyond the state-specified amount the person in care is allowed to have. (In 2011, the person in care was allowed to have $2,000 in a checking or savings account.)

- In some states, if income falls below the poverty line for a family of two, the community spouse may receive additional allowances from the income of the other spouse, who is referred to as the "institutionalized spouse."

- If housing costs for the community spouse are excessive, or if other dependents of the institutionalized spouse live with the community spouse, additional allowances may be made.

- If there is a married couple and the spouse is not living in the nursing home, they will not be required to become destitute in order to pay for care; however, some states now require a "payback" for care after that spouse has died.

- When a "payback" is required, the state will bill the estate after the spouse of the institutionalized person dies.

Gifting Money

Medicaid rules do not allow people to "gift away" money to anyone (children, grandchildren, etc.) in order to qualify. Medicaid enforces a strict five-year "look-back" period. If money was transferred or "gifted" during the past five years, there will be a penalty. This often causes a delay in Medicaid eligibility.

Medicaid and Property Ownership

Let's gain a clearer understanding of the term "assets," especially as it applies to property ownership. If a person's home does not qualify as an exempt asset because its allotted property value is too high, it must be spent down. In other words, the house in good faith must be listed for sale with the intent of the net proceeds after the sale be given to Medicaid for incurred care expense. There are strict federal and state rules with written procedures for this process so the patient can be in compliance and qualify for Medicaid nursing home benefits. However, if the value of the applicant's house exceeds the Medicaid allowable limit but is held in a trust, it is not counted as an asset. Medicaid does not include the value of "non-countable" assets in the applicant's financial net worth equation. The home of the applicant and the property it sits on are not counted as assets as long as a spouse, dependent child, or disabled relative lives there. (Some states may have a cap on the dollar amount of the house and property value. Most people who are attempting to qualify for Medicaid are nowhere close to the cap.) If the house is vacant, the house is still *not* counted as an asset if the Medicaid applicant (or a family member speaking on his or her behalf) expresses a desire to return to the family home. (This is the case even if this is an unrealistic desire, and there is no chance of the patient's returning home.)

If the property is used for income, it is subject to an income-producing rule. The rule states that any real and tangible personal property is exempt if and only if it produces a 6 percent or less net profit. This rule does *not* apply to any type of liquid asset like cash, gold coins, or checking/savings accounts. If the applicant, or the individual who is financially responsible for the applicant, uses the property in any form of business or trade, it is exempt, regardless of its value and amount of profit. The caveat is that this person must be actively involved in the operation of the business on a daily basis. Property that is considered exempt in this case includes land, buildings that are necessary to produce income, operating capital and any assets required to generate the income, such as equipment, livestock, vehicles, inventory and liquid assets, as long as they are not intertwined with personal funds.

If the applicant has real estate and equipment that are used solely to produce goods or services for the home, they are considered exempt. Examples of this would be land that is used for gardening to provide food for home consumption, as well as tractors, gardening tools, etc. If the property in question is not currently being used to produce goods and services for personal use, but has been used for that purpose within the past 12 months and will be used in this manner within the next 12 months, it is still an exempt asset.

Property that cannot be sold is not counted as an asset. This may occur when:

1. The owner of the property is mentally incompetent and legally considered incapable of selling the property.

2. There is a problem regarding the title of the property.

3. The property has been for sale for a long period of time. In this instance, when the property in question finally does sell, it will be counted as an asset and Medicaid coverage may be interrupted until those funds are spent and the person can become eligible again.

Property can be tricky, especially in today's economy. Certain types of property may not be countable assets when the applicant applies. After both spouses have died, however, some states can claim the property as repayment for nursing-home care. It does get complicated. That's why it's best to discuss this with your eldercare attorney. He or she can educate you regarding the best ways to reallocate assets.

The above property acid tests can be avoided by having all properties titled in the name of the applicant's trust. Then, the trust owns all the property, and the trustee manages the property. When this is done, the property is uncountable and exempt as an asset.

HOW TO QUALIFY

General Medicaid Qualification Guidelines

Here are some rules to remember when reallocating assets for Medicaid qualification:

- If a Medicaid applicant is married, assets titled in the applicant's name, the spouse's name, or both names will be counted.
- Jointly held property may not be counted if the property cannot be sold.
- Prepaid funerals, burial plots, monuments, and markers or headstones are not counted as assets. Some states allow the applicant to pay not only for her own funeral in advance, but also her spouse's, children's and grandchildren's, and none will be counted as an asset. Each state may have a maximum amount that an individual can set aside in an irrevocable trust. Your local funeral home or preplanning professional or caseworker will be able to tell you these amounts. (The Appendix discusses preplanning a funeral.)
- Personal possessions are not counted as assets unless they have a large value on them. An example of this would be a gold coin collection.
- Joint bank accounts are counted as assets.

Qualifying for Medicaid assistance can be an overwhelming and arduous task. The facts and guidelines are difficult to understand, and they are different for every state. But by reading this book and completing the Family Care Plan at the end of each chapter, you have already given yourself an advantage. You may not be an expert, but you now have the knowledge needed to ask the experts the right questions.

KEY POINT

Qualifying for Medicaid is a process, not an event.

Why Reposition Your Assets

We've covered the need to reposition your or your loved one's assets in order to maintain a financial legacy for loved ones and still qualify for Medicaid. The following examples show what can happen to someone's assets if he or she fails to reposition her assets prior to requesting Medicaid assistance and completing the Medicaid application.

Some states have a few nuances that may change these examples slightly. However, the end result will be similar. If you are not proactive, here's what to expect.

Example 1:

Single person, age 74, can no longer live at home. Three adult children and four grandchildren. Assets consists of:

- House (appraised value—$125,000)
- Car (appraised value—$5,000)
- Social security ($800 monthly)
- Checking and savings (combined—$25,000)
- Pension ($1,000 monthly)
- Antique doll collection (valued at over $5,000)
- 100 shares of company stock worth $2 a share purchased at 35 cents a share
- Term life insurance ($5,000)
- Whole life insurance (death benefit of $15,000 and cash surrender value of $7,500)

In order to meet Medicaid qualifications, this person can have only:

- $2,000 in assets
- Irrevocable funeral plan ($11,450; can do one per direct-blood-line family member)
- Term life insurance of $5,000

Everything else must be sold or depleted in order for this person to be eligible for the cost of care. Nothing can be gifted to family or relatives. Why? Because the person in need of care does not have a living spouse or underage dependent who is in need of a place to live or transportation. If this individual enters into a care facility on Medicaid, he or she is not healthy enough to return home and will no longer need to drive. The government will be responsible for any food, shelter, and required medical transportation.

Example 2:

Married couple, applicant is age 82 and spouse is age 77, blended family consists of four adult children and 12 grandchildren. Assets consist of:

- Primary residence in Michigan (appraised value of $180,000)
- Lake cottage in northern Indiana (appraised at $150,000)
- Six weeks joint ownership of condo in the Florida (appraised at $25,000)
- Two weeks joint ownership of condo in Colorado (appraised at $5,000)
- Applicant's IRA ($70,000)
- Spouse IRA ($35,000)
- Applicant whole life insurance (cash surrender value $100,000)
- Spouse whole life insurance (cash surrender $50,000)
- Applicant's car (appraised at $15,000)
- Spouse's car (appraised at $28,000)
- Pontoon boat (appraised at $5,000)
- Golf cart (appraised at $3,000)
- Jointly held mutual funds ($185,000)
- Certificate of deposit ($20,000)
- Joint checking and savings ($50,000)
- Combined social security income ($3,200 monthly)
- Applicant term insurance ($10,000)
- Vintage antique gun collection (appraised at $25,000)

Based on 2010-2011 Medicaid guidelines, the applicant is clearly able to pay for care and still support the healthy spouse. However, the average cost of a monthly stay in a nursing home is approximately $6,500. The life expectancy of the healthy spouse is age 86.8, or just short of 10 more years (based on http://longevity.about.com/od/longevity101/p/life_expect.htm). To enable the spouse to continue living in the manner to which he or she is accustomed, assets will have to be reallocated. Otherwise the couple is at risk of having to deplete their assets until they have only:

- One house
- One vehicle
- $2,000 for the applicant
- Maximum of the state of MI's spousal allowance ($109,560 in 2010)
- Irrevocable funeral plan average $11,450 (Each state varies with this figure. This is the average. Verify your state at http://www.cms.gov/MedicaidEligibility/downloads/ListStateMedicaidWebsites.pdf)
- Burial space items (monument or marker)
- Personal items
- Term life insurance

Everything else must be sold, repositioned, or depleted in order to be eligible for the cost of care. Nothing can be gifted to family or relatives.

Remember to Do the Math!

Let's do the math. For a person aged 75 about to enter a nursing home

- 2009 average cost per day to stay $216.66
- Daily stay of $216.66 x 30 days = $6,500 a month
- $6,500.00 a month x 12 months in a year = $78,000 a year
- $73,200 a year x 3 (the average stay) = $234,000

It doesn't take long to burn through a person's life savings, regardless of his or her net worth. You must ask yourself if you want to risk everything your loved one has worked his entire life for. Or do you want to preserve as much as legally possible? It all comes down to this question: What's your level of risk tolerance?

By working within the parameters of the law and using the right financial tools, many people successfully rearrange their loved one's assets in a way that will not expose them to loss when meeting Medicaid qualifications. Medicaid will then pay for most, if not all, nursing home expenses that are normal and customary.

It's Time to Qualify for Medicaid; Now What Do I Do?

Once you have determined that care is necessary, the first thing to do is find a qualified care facility. The nursing home or care facility you choose must be Medicaid-certified.

Many of them have admittance coordinators or social workers who will provide you with the necessary paperwork and point you in the right direction for Medicaid assistance. Otherwise, you'll have to stop by (in person or online) your county's Department of Human Services office and request the paperwork. Regardless of where the help comes from, it is now time to complete all the paperwork required to qualify for Medicaid.

To qualify for Medicaid, your loved one will be required to meet a *means test*. This is where income and assets must be under a predetermined amount, dictated by the state of residence. A Medicaid caseworker will be assigned to the application and will investigate your or your loved one's financial status in order to make an eligibility determination.

Below are some rules to remember:

1. If the applicant is widowed or single, he will be allowed only $2,000 in assets.
2. If there is a spouse, an asset declaration form will need to be completed.
3. If the applicant's income exceeds the state's guideline, he will have to enter into care as a private pay resident until his assets are spent down.
4. The applicant's income includes Social Security benefits, pension benefits, and veteran's benefits.
5. If the spouse works, there is no limit on the income he or she can earn; however, the spouse cannot give the applicant money or it will be considered income.

Each state varies regarding items that may be deducted when calculating the applicant's monthly income. Following are the criteria in most states:

1. $60 for personal needs
2. Health insurance premiums paid by the applicant
3. Up to $60 per guardian, conservator fees, or costs
4. Spousal allowance (formula will be discussed later)
5. Allowance for applicant's dependents or spouse's dependents living at home (dollar limits are subject to change at any time, so check with your county for the current limits)

There is no room for error on any item requested by the Department of Human Services in the Medicaid assistance qualification process. The burden of proof is on you to show that the applicant's assets meet the guidelines. The caseworker will not make any assumptions.

KEY POINT

Keep every receipt and all statements and create a paper trail so that if there are any questions, you can respond accordingly and not jeopardize eligibility.

If an applicant fails to pass the means test, he or she can reapply for Medicaid to pay for nursing home care once his or her assets are depleted. Depleting one's assets (spending down) allows the applicant to pay medical expenses, living costs, and other bills and to purchase things that are considered non-countable assets.

Upon approval, Medicaid will send a letter with their decision. Medicaid will pay only for the services that they deem necessary; the balance of services must be paid for by the patient.

If you have completed the Family Care Plans at the end of each chapter, you are in a good position to begin qualification for Medicaid.

Qualifying for Medicaid is not just completing the form provided by the caseworker at the Department of Human Services or the nursing home. It's about beginning with the end in mind. Reposition your loved one's assets to play by the rules.

Family Care Plan

As previously stated, qualifying for Medicaid is not just completing the necessary forms—it's about understanding the process and creating a custom plan to protect the person's asset base in order to be in legal compliance. Outside of the forms that you will receive from the Department of Human Resources or a case worker, you'll want to take inventory of the below items. If you don't have them completed now, don't worry; however, by the time you need to qualify for Medicaid, they will be necessary.

Once everything is completed, should you elect to take this to a knowledgeable eldercare attorney, the path to qualifying for Medicaid is a short one. Overall expense and fees to have your attorney complete the paperwork for your compliance will significantly decrease (if things were completed properly), and the cumbersome requirements and hoops for Medicaid qualification will have been, or will very quickly be, met.

FAMILY CARE PLAN

The following is a checklist of what will need to be completed or fulfilled. Please mark with a check mark what is finished, so you know on a go-forward basis what will need to be done.

1. _____Living Will for medical purposes
2. _____Specifics on end-of-life support and/or heroic measures
3. _____Do Not Resuscitate Order
4. _____Organ Donation
5. _____Durable Power of Attorney-Medical
   Where is it located? _____
   Who has copies? _____

6. _____Durable Power of Attorney-Financial
   Where is it located? _____
   Who has copies? _____

7. _____Living Trust with Contingent Trustees
   Where is it located? _____
   Who has copies? _____

8. Yes / No   Is the Trust properly funded? Are all of the contents that were placed into the Trust titled properly so that the "Trust" has ownership and not the individual(s)?

9. _____Funeral plan—irrevocably funded.
10. _____Funeral plan for spouse—irrevocably funded.
11. _____Funeral plans for blood children/grandchildren.
12. _____Burial Space Exclusion laws—marker/monument

Who completed the above funeral arrangements for you?

Name: _____

13. What funeral home do you prefer? _____

14. Is there a cemetery you prefer or at which you own property? _____
_____

15. Where are the funeral and cemetery documents located?   _____
_____

16. Who has copies? _____

17. ____Last Will & Testament
    • Make sure items pass through the proper legal entities to avoid as
      much probate tax as possible.

18. Double-check beneficiaries on financial asset items to match the living
    trust.
    Where are these documents located? _____
    Who has copies? _____

CHAPTER 4:

UNDERSTANDING LIFE INSURANCE

In this chapter you will learn:

1. What life insurance is and isn't
2. The types of life insurance
3. How life insurance factors into eldercare decisions

RUSS AND YVONNE

Time for a Change

Every Friday, Russ and Yvonne had the same routine. They would get up and play double solitaire while watching the news and sharing a pot of coffee. Then they would head out for Yvonne's hair appointment. Then it was to The Greeks downtown for lunch. They had had this routine for years.

Often while Russ was waiting for his wife's appointment to be over, he'd walk across the street to the barbershop to catch up on the local news. Or if he were hungry, he'd wander down to the corner gas station to buy a doughnut and eat it on his way back to the beauty shop, where he would patiently wait until his wife was finished.

This Friday, Russ went to talk to the men. Yvonne waved and called out, "Enjoy! I'll walk over when I'm done." Russ smiled and began walking. Yvonne was happy to enjoy an hour with just the girls. Afterwards, she tipped her stylist and walked across the street to the barbershop. When she got there, the guys said that Russ had stopped in, but had seemed preoccupied. He had had a cup of joe and headed out the door.

"He must have wanted a doughnut," she mumbled to herself and headed to the gas station, only to learn Russ hadn't been there. Russ was predictable—like clockwork. This wasn't normal. Trying not to panic, Yvonne began to look for him, cursing herself for quietly accepting and hiding his memory struggles.

For the first time, Yvonne admitted to herself that she may have to talk to their families about Russ's difficulties sooner rather than later. She burst into tears when she finally found Russ waiting for her in the front passenger seat of their car.

"Hey, Kid, why the tears? Your hair looks great!" he said. "I'm hungry, let's get lunch."

Yvonne sighed and felt silly for panicking. She tried to convince herself that she had simply misunderstood where he said he was going. Deep down, she knew she hadn't. Regardless, it was time for lunch, and food always made everything better. As they walked into The Greeks, they bumped into their friend and insurance and investment advisor, Bob. He mentioned that he would be calling them soon since it was time again to review their entire portfolio. Yvonne felt like he had read her mind. Yes, it was time to review their portfolio—and the sooner the better. While Russ was somewhat in sound mind, she needed to make sure that all their legal and medical documents were current.

When they got home, Russ went to the sun porch to watch the *Masters*. Yvonne went in and handed him some lemonade. "Sit, relax, enjoy golf," she said. "I'm going to do some paperwork in the office."

Yvonne went to work on the pile of bills that was waiting for her. As she sifted through the mail, she noticed an advertisement in the newspaper for their attorney, encouraging people to come to his office and make out a will. She took this as a sign from above and decided to make an appointment to update everything, including their durable powers of attorney and their patient advocate and living will forms, all of which had never been updated or, for that matter, even reviewed. So many things had changed since they had first had those documents drawn up. It was time to revisit them, and Yvonne was looking forward to checking this off her list of to-dos.

Later that next week, Yvonne and Russ were in the attorney's office reviewing their advocacy forms. The attorney pointed out that there was not a second person listed on either of their durable powers of attorney papers—just each other. This was a matter for concern because it left them vulnerable should something happen to the two of them simultaneously. Neither one of them would be able to speak for the other, let alone for him or herself. No one legally could be their voice. The attorney recommended that each of them add one of their children as a contingent person who would be able to sign on the parent's behalf with a durable power of attorney for medical and financial affairs.

Last but not least, the attorney suggested something new. Years ago, when their documents had been prepared, medical technology had not been as advanced as it was today. Medical advancements could now save or prolong life, whereas it couldn't have done so even ten years ago. What medical science couldn't guarantee was quality of life.

The attorney asked Russ and Yvonne to be clear on what procedures or heroic measures, if any, they would want done for themselves in the case of a medical emergency. For example, would they want to be placed on a ventilator if that was required to save their life?

They both thought this was a great idea and shared that neither of them wanted to be a "vegetable" on artificial life support with no hope for recovery or independent lifestyle. They even went so far as to put a "Do Not Resuscitate" order in their files. They carried a copy with them in case something should happen. These documents were being drafted as they were leaving, and a second appointment was set for them to come in and review their last will and testaments.

Their visit with the attorney had been on Tuesday. That Friday, Yvonne dropped Russ off at her son's house so that he could go on a boat ride. Russ loved pontoon rides and looked forward to spending time with his son and grandson.

He enjoyed just hanging out and being one of the guys. Besides, with Yvonne not around, he could tell a few fish tales while he had an ice-cold beer on the boat.

Yvonne waved goodbye as she pulled out of the driveway and headed to her doctor's appointment. A few weeks ago, she and Russ had gone in for their annual checkups, and the office had called and asked if she wouldn't mind coming in for a consult by herself.

* * *

Life insurance was invented by the ancient Romans, who formed "burial clubs" to share and defray the cost of funerals. Modern life insurance was created in England during the seventeenth century.

—LifeQuote.com

Most of our parents and older relatives, as well as most members of the Boomer generation, have life insurance policies if they were actively employed throughout their working lives. They may have retired and purchased insurance at a reduced rate, or their parents may have purchased it for them when they were children. Many times they have term insurance provided by the company from which they retired.

ELDERCARE DECISIONS REGARDING LIFE INSURANCE

When it comes to end-of-life planning, the type of insurance a person has can greatly impact his or her ability to qualify for Medicaid. Understand what type of policy the person in need of care has in force so that his or her assets can be repositioned when the time comes. It's important to read the fine print; just because the term "life insurance" is printed on a document doesn't mean a death benefit will necessarily be paid. That will depend on the type of life insurance.

When you discover a life insurance policy when planning for long-term care for a loved one, refer to the Family Care Plan at the end of this chapter. It lists facts you need to find out about the policy. Once you have uncovered the facts, you'll have a better handle on how to proceed.

WHAT LIFE INSURANCE IS NOT
Accidental Death and Dismemberment

Accidental death and dismemberment insurance is also referred to as "AD&D." AD&D claims are paid only when the death of the insured is a result of an accident or when the insured loses a limb due to an accident. People often sign up for this form of insurance through a credit card company or bank without realizing that the benefit is paid only if death is the result of an accident. An accidental death must be declared by a medical examiner or coroner. These types of policies are black and white. More times than not, a person's death is not accident-related, and the insurance company will not pay the claim.

Company-Sponsored Death Benefits

In our parents' generation many companies set up self-funded insurance-type policies or certificates for their retirees.

In these cases, a company developed its own set of rules for a retirement program, with one of the benefits being a burial or death benefit for the retiree. The policy documentation will have specific instructions to contact a designated human resource department or benefits manager upon the death of the retired employee.

ONE WAY

Do not confuse life insurance with accidental death and dismemberment policies. They are two entirely separate forms of insurance coverage.

It is common for these certificates to stipulate a payout in the form of a flat stipend or fee. For example, the certificate might have a death benefit consisting of a lump sum of $2,000. Some group term certificates may have a decreasing benefit based on age. Much like a decreasing term life policy, the benefit may be $5,000 at age 65 and only $2,000 at age 80. These types of benefits have no cash value and are not considered to be an asset for the retiree.

You must verify whether this benefit is still in force. When companies close, consolidate, or are sold, retiree programs are often discontinued.

KEY POINT

Many employers offer term life insurance coverage as a benefit to employees. Often this coverage continues to be in force for the retiree as a retirement benefit.

WHAT LIFE INSURANCE IS

Life insurance is a contract between an individual and a life insurance company. The individual pays a set premium on a regular basis in exchange for a pre-determined settlement that will be paid to a designated beneficiary upon that individual's death.

Life-insurance-agent and financial-planner positions have high turnover. Why? Because it takes working nights, evenings, and even weekends to build a solid business. Not all people are willing to work non-conventional hours and to invest their time in building relationships with people.

Many insurance agents and financial planners hold their positions for fewer than two years. There are many reputable, seasoned, and trusted people in this profession; just remember to check references and trust your instincts. Don't just change your insurance agent or financial planner because a company's portfolio looks appealing—ask the professional with whom you've done business to make the comparison for you.

Premiums are typically determined through an industry-established actuarial table that takes into account factors such as age, gender, health, whether a person smokes, and how active he or she is. The original intent of insurance was twofold:

- To pay for the insured's funeral
- To provide income for those dependent on the insured's paycheck

Almost since the insurance industry's beginnings, variations on these goals have appeared. Today, people often buy life insurance policies for reasons that have nothing to do with their original purpose.

The Evolution of Life Insurance

Over the years, life insurance has gone from a means of paying for one's funeral to being an investment vehicle or an income supplement for survivors of the deceased. For this reason, life-insurance companies offer many types of products to assist customers with their financial goals.

There are three basic types of life insurance. Of these three types, variable life is the most complex.

Term Insurance

Term insurance is the least expensive form of protection. It provides coverage for only a specified number of years—such as 5, 10, or 20. At the end of the term, the insurance expires, and another policy must be purchased. If the insured dies while the policy is in force, the death benefit (sometimes referred to as the "face amount" or "policy limit") is paid to the beneficiary in one lump sum. These death benefits are tax-free. The premiums are determined at the time of purchase and are paid over a specified period of time. The payments may also be structured to increase or decrease over time. If an existing policy expires, a new policy will typically require a higher premium, even though the death benefit remains unchanged, since the insured will then be older. Term insurance carries no cash value.

Whole Life Insurance

Whole life insurance is insurance with a savings account attached. Premiums for whole life are usually a fixed dollar amount over a set time period—usually the insured's "whole life," or close to it—and are higher than term life policies. These policies have a minimum cash value, which grows tax-deferred at a guaranteed rate over time. This cash value is like a savings account. If the insured decides to cancel the account prior to death, he or she will be paid this amount (in this case, it is sometimes referred to as the "cash surrender value"), and the policy will no longer be in force. A cash surrender may trigger a tax liability.

The insured can also borrow against the cash value and need not ever repay the loan since he or she has essentially borrowed the money from him or herself. Of course, if the loan is not repaid, the death benefit will be lower. Upon the insured's death, the insurance company will recover the loan amount plus interest. Thus the beneficiary will receive the difference between the face value of the policy and the recovered loan. This beneficiary does not have to pay federal income taxes on the payout, but the death benefit must be included in the estate's assets when calculating estate taxes.

Whole life policies are usually purchased both to pay for funeral expenses and to leave a financial legacy for loved ones.

Universal Life Insurance

Universal life policies offer more flexibility than regular whole life insurance. The client can adjust both the death benefit and the premium. He or she can elect to pay a higher premium if a greater benefit is desired or decrease the premium for less coverage, saving money in the process. The insured can also cease paying premiums and allow the cash value of the policy to cover the payments, assuming there is a sufficient cash value to do so. As with traditional whole life insurance, the cash value is

Universal life insurance policies vary greatly. It's critical to understand surrender options as well as penalties when considering the decision to surrender the policy or take out a policy loan.

guaranteed to grow at a specified minimum rate The premiums are deposited in the general account of the company, and the cash value may grow at a substantially higher rate if the investments in that account do well. However, regardless of how poorly the investments do, the cash value and death benefit are guaranteed by the insurance company.

INVESTMENT INSURANCES

Variable Insurance

Variable insurance is usually purchased as an investment vehicle rather than an end-of-life policy for funeral expenses. People who can afford to take a higher risk may purchase this type of insurance to hold in their investment portfolios. In many ways, variable insurance resembles life insurance, but don't let the word insurance fool you—it's not insurance like we just learned about. It's an investment vehicle. For an agent to sell a "variable insurance policy" he or she must have a life insurance license *and* a securities license.

The premiums paid for variable life policies are invested in what is called a "separate account," rather than in the insurance company's general account, and the cash values and death benefits are dependent on the returns earned by the invested premiums. The insured selects which of the separate account's "sub-accounts" his or her premiums will be invested in, and if these accounts perform poorly, the cash value of the policy might even be zero, which means that the insured would receive nothing if he or she chose to surrender the policy. The death benefit will also vary with the performance of the investment portfolios selected; however, there is a minimum guaranteed death benefit (a floor) associated with these policies. A portion of the premium does get deposited into the general account, out of which this guaranteed death benefit is paid.

KEY POINT

With variable life policies, the premium is fixed; however the cash value is not guaranteed. Both the cash value and the death benefit are tied to the success or failure of the investment portfolio. The cash value may be zero if the portfolio has suffered negative returns, but there is a minimum guaranteed death benefit, often referred to as a floor, that will be paid regardless of how poorly the portfolio performs.

Variable Universal Life

Unlike universal and whole life insurance accounts, variable universal life allows you to separate your cash accounts into more than one account for investment purposes. It typically requires you to manage your investments or to pay a fee for company management. In a nutshell, risk is on your shoulders based on what investments you make.

Dave Ramsey, a popular financial guru and syndicated radio talk show host (http://www.daveramsey.com/article/the-truth-about-life-insurance/) believes that term insurance is the only way to go. Why? Ramsey believes that the only

ONE WAY

Term insurance, whole life insurance, and universal life insurance are strictly insurance products because the insurance company is bearing the investment risk. Variable life and variable universal life insurance are classified as securities because the insured is bearing the investment risk.

reason a person should have life insurance is to take care of the surviving spouse and to pay off any debt. However, not all term insurance policies are alike. Many times people think they have term insurance but what they really have is a "decreasing term policy." These policies lose value each year until they essentially provide no coverage after a certain age. These policies have no cash value and do not affect qualification for Medicaid.

Ramsey also reports that if people don't have term coverage, they tend to have whole life insurance, which has some form of cash value. On average, these policies have a face amount of $25,000 or less. This is problematic when the insured is entering a long-term care facility and attempting to qualify for Medicaid. According to Ramsey, more than 70 percent of the insurance

Cash value is the amount received by the insured upon cancellation of an insurance policy. It is also referred to as surrender value.

policies still being sold today are whole life. They are appealing to people because they have a built-in savings account. People purchase these with the intent to retire with some added wealth. What they don't realize is that the growth of these policies is so minimal that they would be better off purchasing a larger term insurance policy for the difference in premium. Also, as we live longer it is more likely that we'll need long-term care, and the cash value of the policy becomes problematic when applying for Medicaid.

KEY POINT

This area is one in which a good eldercare attorney or experienced funeral planning professional (or both) will be beneficial!

Note: It's best to compare answers between the eldercare attorney and the funeral planning professionals.

Our Insurance Has Cash Value. Now What?

When qualifying your loved one for Medicaid, the cash value of his or her life insurance policy must not be more than $1,500. When the cash value exceeds $1,500 you have four options:

1. Do nothing and know that this will make the person in need of care ineligible for Medicaid, resulting in a private-pay scenario.

2. Surrender the insurance policy and receive whatever cash value has accrued within the policy, which may result in tax consequences for the policy owner and will result in the loss of the death benefit to the beneficiary. Simply said, the policy will no longer be in force.

> Your eldercare attorney and your funeral planning professional may not be on the same page. If you learn that the advice you receive from each of them conflicts, don't try to be the middleman. Instead, don't panic, but ask for them to communicate with each other, as laws can change regularly.

3. Eliminate the insurance policy's cash value through the use of an insurance transaction called a 1035 exchange. A 1035 exchange will eliminate any tax consequences for the policy owner. A 1035 exchange is where one insurance policy's cash surrender value is "exchanged" or transferred to form a new life insurance policy, therefore sheltering the owner of the policy from any tax consequences. There are certain restrictions when using a 1035 exchange; your insurance agent, eldercare attorney, or funeral planning professional will understand when this is a viable option. A licensed insurance agent can process this with either the policy owner or caregiver who holds a durable power of attorney.

4. Eliminate the cash value by borrowing against it. This keeps the policy intact until the insured's death. The policy owner or the individual with a durable power of attorney can complete this transaction with the assistance of the insurance company's customer service department. When death occurs and a death claim is filed, the loan is paid back, along with any interest, by being deducted from the death benefit. The difference is paid to the policy's beneficiary.

If you want your loved one to qualify for Medicaid, funds acquired through an insurance policy loan should be allocated to assets that are defined as exempt in your state's Medicaid rules. Keep receipts on all transaction because you may be required to show your paper trail.

This also applies if the insured has an investment policy (annuity). An expert eldercare attorney may recommend a different strategy.

The following Family Care Plan will guide you through the discovery process and help you to understand what your loved one has.

FAMILY CARE PLAN

You may have to do a lengthy scavenger hunt on behalf your loved one. Look for all life insurance policies and riders—like accidental death and dismemberment insurance—he or she has in force.

Remember, just because a person tells you he has no life insurance doesn't mean that there isn't any. He may have a policy in force that he is unaware of.

You may need a date of birth, Social Security number and even a durable power of attorney to obtain the answers if you have to call a previous employer or an insurance company. Don't be alarmed; this is standard practice in today's workplace due to privacy regulations.

Are there any life insurance policies?   Yes   No
If yes, continue answering the questions below.

What type of policy?

A.	Retirement from an employer	Yes	No
B.	Term Life	Yes	No
C.	Whole Life	Yes	No
D.	Variable Life/investment insurance	Yes	No
E.	Accidental Death/Dismemberment ONLY	Yes	No
F.	Accidental Death/Dismemberment as a rider	Yes	No

Is there an employee retirement benefit insurance policy?   Yes   No
If yes, continue answering the questions below.

A. What company/employer did this come from?

Company name: _____

Company telephone number: _____

Company email address: _____

Company mailing address: _____

B. Are there instructions for what to do upon death and/or how to file a death claim?

                                                                     Yes   No

C. Does it list the policy's primary beneficiary?   Yes   No

      If yes, who: _____

D. Has the company moved, changed its name, or been sold to another business?

      If so, list:

      New company name: _____

      New company telephone number: _____

      New company email address: _____

      New company mailing address: _____

> **STOP**
>
> If the company your loved one worked for has closed, look for any letters or communication from them. Companies are required by law to notify all employees and retirees who have any form of benefits of what the intentions are regarding the benefits. If benefits were discontinued there should be a notification. Otherwise, contact the insurance agency or company that provided the benefits. The worst that can happen is that there is no coverage.

If all you find is a copy or a receipt from an employer referencing a plan of this type and no documentation or instructions:

Contact the company's human resource department and ask the following questions (be sure to have the policy, the retiree's date of birth and Social Security number on hand):

Is the benefit of this policy is still in force?   Yes   No

For whom? (Are there additional beneficiaries?) _____

How is a death claim submitted? _____

FAMILY CARE PLAN

If it's not a privately held employer retiree benefit:

1. By what insurance company is it written? (For example, Principal, Metropolitan)

   _____

2. Who is the insurance agent/agency? _____
   Telephone: _____

Don't know? Search online for the website of the insurance company
and call their customer service department (be sure to have the policy on hand).

Whether the policy is from an insurance company or an employer retiree benefit, ask if the policy or benefit is:

Term	Yes	No
Decreasing term	Yes	No
Whole Life	Yes	No
Variable	Yes	No
Other (explain):		
Does the policy expire at certain age or number of years?	Yes	No

If so, when? _____

What is the face amount? _____

What is the death benefit? _____

Who is the primary beneficiary? _____

Are there secondary or multiple beneficiaries?	Yes	No

If yes, who (and what is the percentage for each individual)?

_____

FAMILY CARE PLAN

If the policy is any form of whole life or investment insurance ask the following questions:

Is there any cash value attached to the policy?   Yes   No

Does the insurance policy have an outstanding policy loan against it?

                                                               Yes   No

If yes, how much is the loan? _____

What is the interest rate? _____

What are the terms (if any) for repayment? _____

(If payments are still being made via pension or policy dividends, do you want to keep the policy in force?)

Is there any Accidental Death/Dismemberment attached to the policies?

                                                               Yes   No

How do you file a death claim?_____

Check to see if any of your loved one's credit cards have life insurance attached to the account—some do.

Is your parent or loved one a member of a credit union?   Yes   No

If yes, ask if the credit union has any free insurance on their members.

                                                               Yes   No

If yes, ask for an explanation of coverage.

Is there a long-term care (LTC) insurance policy?   Yes   No

If yes, with what company? _____

FAMILY CARE PLAN

Call the company's customer service department or agent and ask the following questions:

Is the policy still in force?	Yes	No
Are there in-home benefits?	Yes	No
Unlimited benefits/coverage?	Yes	No
Is there a maximum number of days of care?	Yes	No

If yes, the maximum is: _____

Are there deductibles or co-payments?	Yes	No

If yes, how much? _____

Single or private room? _____

Skilled or non-skilled assisted care or nursing-home facility?

_____

Are prescriptions included?	Yes	No
Are there deductibles or co-payments?	Yes	No

If yes, how much? _____

How are claims submitted? _____

Chapter 5:
End-of-Life Healthcare and
Financial Directives

In this chapter you will learn:

1. How to be a healthcare advocate for your parent or loved one
2. How to prepare healthcare advance directives
3. How to regain control

Russ and Yvonne

A Marker Moment

Yvonne had forgotten that she had a doctor's appointment until she heard a courtesy reminder call on their answering machine. She assumed that she and the doctor would review the results of her annual physical, which included lab work, stress tests, and a chest x-ray. Second, she was sure they would discuss Russ. All in all, she thought things would be predictable and straightforward.

She liked their internist, Dr. Foster; he was young, thorough, and empathetic. She especially appreciated that he would break protocol when he felt it was necessary. She and Russ had been patients of his for the last six years. They had come to think of Dr. Foster as a friend and trusted his judgment.

Dr. Foster greeted her with his usual charm and then got right down to business. He liked to spend as much time with each patient as possible but realized that his time was limited.

Yvonne sat down, expecting to get a clean bill of health before the discussion turned to Russ's odd behavior of late. Instead, she was blindsided. Nothing could have prepared her for what she was about to hear.

"Let's take a look at your chest x-ray," Dr. Foster said. "I'm concerned because the right lung appears to be larger than the left. See the difference in coloring between them? If my suspicions are correct, you have the beginning stages of emphysema. I know you thought your breathing issues were allergy-related, but the underlying problem may be emphysema. I'd like to conduct a few more tests to confirm this. I also want to adjust your meds and teach you how to do home breathing treatments."

Yvonne listened with a blank stare. Dr. Foster asked her a question. Yvonne didn't respond. Instead she burst into tears. Dr. Foster hugged her and let her cry. He knew that Yvonne wasn't crying about her health; she was crying out of fear for Russ.

For months, she, Russ, and Dr. Foster had been dancing around the official diagnosis of dementia. Before sitting Russ down to discuss his formal diagnosis, Dr. Foster had had an off-the-record conversation with Yvonne. He asked Yvonne to record Russ's memory mishaps, behaviors, and appetite in a journal with daily or at least weekly entries. The entries didn't have to be lengthy—just dates and bullet points to determine patterns. Dr. Foster knew that this activity would help Yvonne, too, since journaling is often therapeutic for caregivers. This type of "homework" also prepares the partner emotionally for a pending diagnosis, enabling at least one party to stay composed when the diagnosis is discussed with the patient.

Dr. Foster had asked Yvonne to bring the journal to Russ's next routine office visit. (He had quarterly appointments because of his prescriptions.) Dr. Foster knew he was breaking client-patient privacy rules. With some patients, however, he was guided by his internal compass, not policy.

Now, Yvonne pulled herself together enough to ask Dr. Foster what the next steps were and to schedule the next appointment. Then she got into the car, opened the glove compartment, grabbed her cigarettes, and tossed them out the window.

So many things went racing through her mind. Now she felt an even greater sense of urgency to get their personal and financial affairs in order. Yvonne's biggest fear and worst nightmare just might come true; there was a real possibility that Russ could outlive her. Who would take care of him? Sure, his children could, but they had their own lives. Becoming a caregiver was a huge responsibility.

Yvonne knew that dementia is an odd disease. Everyone's progression is different. Some people deteriorate quickly; others become shadows of their former selves and linger for years until their heart gives out. Yvonne started to panic. She simply could not wait for next week's appointment with the attorney.

Over the next few days, Yvonne found herself taking inventory. She remembered how Aunt Carol's attorney had helped them with Grandma Ruby. She knew that they had to position themselves financially to prevent losing their house or life savings if either of them should need long-term care. Yvonne knew they had long-term care insurance, but she needed to review exactly what they had purchased. Her list of to-dos grew, and yet she planned on keeping this new secret, as well as the secret of Russ's memory loss, to herself at least for now.

Yvonne realized that the home they lived in was too much for her to care for alone. She also realized that there were long-term financial advantages to owning and not renting if Medicaid ever had to step in.

Within six months, Yvonne and Russ sold their home and moved into a senior condo community. It was perfect. Their new home had all the benefits of their previous one, with less square footage and no yard work. Essentially, it was a gated community for seniors. The move relieved Yvonne tremendously. Russ just said, "If Yvonne's happy, I'm happy."

Once in their new home, Yvonne focused on reallocating their life savings and making sure their family members knew what was going on. She was ready to share their well-kept secret and to quit carrying this load alone. Covering for Russ and hiding her recent diagnosis was becoming difficult to handle.

* * *

"Issues surrounding death and dying are the elephant in the room."
                                    –Stan Goldberg, Ph.D.

This chapter will take a closer look at the legal tools to help you make your loved one's wishes clear and give direction to the medical personnel who are making important medical decisions. These legal documents give your parent or loved one control even when he is no longer able to speak for himself.

END-OF-LIFE MEDICAL OPTIONS

The Patient Advocate

With all the questions raised by end-of-life medical and legal matters, it is easy to see why acting as an advocate for your loved one is essential.

While being an advocate is a true act of love and courage, the initial challenge lies in figuring out how to convince the patient that he or she needs an advocate. Patients, especially aging patients, often feel their privacy is intruded on by having an advocate with them. They may also feel that the advocate is being condescending or even suggesting they are incapable of understanding the information for themselves.

But having a second set of eyes and ears at a doctor's appointment is just common sense. So much important information is shared in a very short period of time and that information must be captured and understood. This is always easier for two people to handle than it is for one.

Furthermore, patients often reject information that is hard to accept. This is human nature. You can help a loved one accept bad news and take steps to face what is to come, even though the diagnosis may be equally hard for you to accept.

The following are some other reasons why having an advocate with a patient is a good idea.

- To ensure that time with the doctor is maximized, and that all health issues are discussed, not just one.

- To ease tension and frustration if a doctor is behind schedule and the patient must sit in the waiting room for a long time. The patient may become annoyed and frustrated, and by the time the doctor (who might also be frustrated and rushed) finally arrives, the patient may be more focused on leaving, or taking her frustration out on the doctor, than on taking the time to discuss the reason for the appointment in the first place.

- To disclose the use of medications that are part of the patient's daily routine, including prescription and over-the-counter drugs, vitamins, and herbal supplements. Research has proven that the risk of adverse side effects and dangerous drug interactions is significantly lower when patients are forthcoming about all of their medications. If you are unsure of your parent's willingness or ability to disclose all of their medications, it will be essential to attend this visit with your parent and act as their advocate.

- To be aware of possible side effects when prescription treatments are changed or altered. The patient often won't recognize subtle behavior changes.

- To ask the doctor the tough questions that the patient may not want to ask.

- To receive all care options including a doctor's perspective enabling a better understanding of the pros and cons of each.

Whenever possible, aging or terminally ill patients should be accompanied through the medical process by an assertive, informed, and dedicated advocate in their corner.

Control Issues

Unfortunately, insurance companies often decide which hospitals, doctors, and medical treatments a patient will have based on what they will or will not pay for. If patients do not agree with the recommendations and want to pursue other avenues or treatments, they must pay for it themselves. Some doctors have stopped practicing medicine because they feel their patient care is compromised because of insurance companies. Some doctors will not accept insurance and make their patients responsible for filing claims, while others have figured out exactly how many patients per day they need to see to be adequately compensated by insurance companies in order to stay in business.

This means that many doctors plan their work days around how many patients they will see and how long they will spend with them. The average practice allows 15 minutes of face time with the doctor; other members of the staff handle duties and assessments that do not require a doctor.

This means that you must take control of the face time your parent has with a physician. Doctors aren't mind readers. They make diagnoses based on medical knowledge, the process of elimination, and what their patient is telling them.

If a doctor seems hurried because he is running behind, that's not your problem! You are entitled to have all your medical questions answered. Do not be rushed! Insist that your loved one's medical needs be addressed.

Advance Directives

There are three different types of advance directives, one of which is strictly asset-related. When all of these documents have been completed they are referred to as *comprehensive advance directives*. Completing directives is by far is the most responsible, proactive thing your loved one can do.

Listed below are the reference documents

1. Living Will/Healthcare Directive, which includes a Do Not Resuscitate order.
2. Durable Power of Attorney (Medical and Financial)
3. Living Trusts (relates to protecting one's assets)

You may wish to assist your loved one in completing these documents or hire an attorney to do it.

As each document is prepared, make sure both your loved one and you understand its purpose, discuss it with the individuals involved, and place it with other important documents. You may want to make copies for family members. Everyone involved will feel a sense of accomplishment and peace of mind.

Most states encourage end-of-life instructions. At the federal government level there are no laws or mandates, leaving all decisions regarding these issues to the states.

Some states will accept advance healthcare directives while others will accept only living wills. Some states will accept both advance healthcare directives and living wills but not Do-No-Resuscitate orders. Other states will accept all three. The burden of understanding what's binding in your parents' state (or the states they frequently travel to) rests on your shoulders or your trusted advisor's. You can find this information on your state's website, at your state's local representative's office or even at the department of human services.

It is not uncommon for an attorney to create both comprehensive advance directives and medical/financial durable powers of attorney as a part of his or her client's initial estate-planning portfolio. But you do not need an attorney to legitimize these documents. If you would like to do it yourself there are several websites that can help you. Some popular ones are www.rocketlawyer.com and www.legacywriter.com. Many of the legal websites request a state of residence and will provide the do-it-yourself, fill-in-the-blank documents that are applicable in your state.

KEY POINT

When researching your state, don't assume a type of advance directive is accepted unless you see the term listed.

Regardless of whether or not your state acknowledges your advance directives, most judges will acknowledge the fact that your wishes were recorded while you were of sound mind and will honor the written documentation as evidence to speak on your behalf.

Make Sure Your Comprehensive Advance Healthcare Directives Includes a Living Will

One of the first items you should attend to is both common and easy to execute—a living will. The term "living will" is often used interchangeably with the term "advance healthcare directive" (or "advance directive"), but there is a subtle difference. Both refer to written documents containing a person's proactive directions regarding her heath care wishes, but a living will focuses on life support while advance healthcare directives focus on healthcare decisions and appoint a patient advocate. Many people confuse the two as one document; however they are separate documents. For the purpose of this discussion we will use the term *comprehensive advance directives* **to refer to both**.

Two fundamental points underscore the importance of comprehensive advance directives:

- Living wills help ensure your right to die with dignity.
- Health-care directives let you determine what path the medical community should follow in the event you are unable to speak for yourself.

Comprehensive advance directives were created as a means to allow ill or injured individuals the ability to speak for themselves. These documents provide the medical community with a Family Care Plan that the patient formulated himself while still of sound mind and body. Comprehensive advance directives can be either general or very specific. The most common directives that are recorded within this document are those regarding life support. Here are some examples of a very specific comprehensive living will:

- The refusal of any lifesaving measures that will prolong life, such as intravenous feedings and mechanical respirators when the individual is dying.
- The refusal of any and all measures taken to prolong life once there is no hope of a medical recovery.
- The refusal of any and all measures that will sustain life with little hope of the individual's return to independent living, equipment-free living, or a quality of life that is similar to that enjoyed before illness or injury.

KEY POINT

Regardless of how specific comprehensive advance directives are, they may still be overruled. With the rapid advances in technology and medical care, some conditions that used to be terminal or life-limiting may quickly become treatable.

Although the advance request is made by the patient, the execution lies solely within the judgment of the medical provider. Most physicians will honor a patient's wishes, but if a medical provider feels new medical treatments may save someone's life and sustain his quality of life within reason, he or she may suggest treatment in opposition to the patient's previous request.

Let's say, for example, someone is severely injured in a car accident. An ambulance rushes to the scene, and he is transported, still unconscious, to the ER.

The person was identified by others who were involved in the accident, and his driver's license was checked. While he is in transit, the emergency personnel

If you completed the comprehensive advance directives on your own, take the extra step to have the documents notarized. While it's not necessary, it lends tremendous credibility.

check to see if his records are in their system so that they will know if he is allergic to any medicines. Previous hospital records verify that the patient has comprehensive advance directives on file stating that he would like no heroic measures to take place in the event he is critically injured and unable to speak for himself. But the wording of the comprehensive advance directives is general. The attending physician needs to make a decision.

If it has not been determined that the patient's situation is permanent or life threatening, the doctor may order the use of an artificial breathing machine until she can determine the long-term prognosis. While this may seem like a heroic measure, it provides a short-term solution for the doctor, allowing her time to make the correct choices regarding the patient's long-term care.

Although comprehensive advance directives should be completed when a person becomes a legal adult, most living wills are completed before a person undergoes a surgical procedure that requires hospitalization. It is not uncommon for a hospital to require a patient to complete or provide one when he or she is admitted. Federal law requires that all persons entering a care facility complete comprehensive advance directives. Comprehensive advance directives are revocable, which means that they can be updated or changed at any time. However, they do not expire.

KEY POINT

Before finalizing a care plan it's always smart to discuss any reservations regarding any "what if" scenarios with your family, physician, and/or attorney and inform them of your wishes both verbally and via your comprehensive advance directives.

Hospitals—and hospital systems—keep living wills on file in case of emergency. If changes have been made to your living will since your last hospital visit, you'll want to update what's on file.

Attention to advance directives will grow as the country continues to debate health care reform. A study of 4.7 million Medicare enrollees found that 30 to 35 percent of Medicare funds are spent on patients with chronic illnesses during the last two years of their lives (The Dartmouth Atlas Project, 2006). These costs represent a sizable opportunity for savings, particularly if monies are being spent on procedures and treatments that do not comply with patient wishes.

Two true stories emphasize the need for comprehensive advance directives. You may remember the Terri Schiavo story. Schiavo collapsed on February 25, 1990, thus beginning 15 years of institutionalization. Her legal case, which lasted from 1998 to 2005, centered on whether Schiavo, diagnosed as being in a persistent vegetative state (PVS), should be kept alive through the use of medical machinery or be allowed to die. After a lengthy court battle much publicity, the court allowed Terry's feeding tube to be removed and she died approximately two weeks later.

Even before Schiavo was Karen Quinlan. Quinlan was the first modern icon of the right-to-die debate. The 21-year-old Quinlan collapsed at a party after swallowing alcohol and tranquilizers on April 14, 1975. Doctors saved her life, but she suffered brain damage and lapsed into a PVS. Her family waged a much-publicized legal battle for the right to remove her life-support machinery. They succeeded, but in a final twist, Quinlan kept breathing after the respirator was unplugged. She remained in a coma for almost 10 years in a New Jersey nursing home until her 1985 death.

To help your family avoid a similar tragic and emotionally devastating situation, create comprehensive advance directives when your loved one is healthy, not when he is sick and emotions are high. If your loved one is in an accident or becomes suddenly ill and unable to speak for himself, medical providers will have no choice but to keep him alive if these documents are not in place.

Every adult—whether single, married, or in a committed relationship—should have comprehensive advance directives. It's not only a great gift of love to those who will have to make excruciating decisions; it's the responsible thing to do.

FIVE WISHES

In 1998, a non-profit advocacy group called Aging with Dignity, working with the Commission on Aging, the American Bar Association, and the support of a grant, created a combined living will and healthcare power of attorney booklet called *Five Wishes*. This document is one of the most accepted and comprehensive resources of its kind. *Five Wishes* was initially intended to be a Florida-only legal document; but through the years it has gained acceptance and legal status in 42 states. It is also available in 26 languages and in Braille. *Five Wishes* is an easy-to-understand booklet that's written in layman terms.

Currently the *Five Wishes* document does not meet these states' legal requirements: Alabama, Indiana, Kansas, New Hampshire, Ohio, Oregon, Texas, and Utah.

Do Not Resuscitate Order (DNR)

A Do Not Resuscitate order is one more type of advance directive that everyone should consider having among his or her important documents. Unlike a living will, this type of directive specifically addresses:

- Cardiopulmonary resuscitation, otherwise referred to as CPR
- Respiratory Arrest

KEY POINT

Five Wishes has been featured on *The Today Show*, in the *Wall Street Journal*, *Time* magazine, the *Washington Post,* and numerous other well-known publications and shows. To learn more about *Five Wishes*, order a copy, or complete one online, go to http:// www.agingwithdignity.org.

Without proof of a Do Not Resuscitate order, sometimes referred to as a *healthcare proxy*, medical professionals will automatically attempt to help all patients who are experiencing cardio or respiratory events and have stopped breathing.

Most people will have only advance directives completed unless they are either terminally ill or have entered a hospital for a surgical procedure. As noted earlier, in most hospitals it's common practice to ask patients to complete a DNR form prior to surgery. In a perfect world, every person would complete a DNR at the age of 18 or 21. DNR forms can be easily obtained from an attorney, at a hospital, or on the Internet (including at my website, www.jodiclock.com).

Do Not Resuscitate (DNR) orders are acknowledged in all states

Durable Power of Attorney

The above discussion has provided you with an idea of what can and has happened when an unexpected illness or accident occurs. Now you have some insight into the short-term and long-term financial ramifications when a person is unable to act or speak for himself. What hasn't been addressed yet is when the personal and financial needs of the incapacitated individual must be taken care of. This is why financial durable power of attorney exists.

ONE WAY →

A durable power of attorney differs from a traditional power of attorney in that the durable power of attorney continues the agency relationship beyond the incapacity of the principal. (www.Legaldictionary. thefreedictionary.com/ Power+of+attorney)

The DPOA appointee, also called an agent, should be a trusted and responsible person who has the patient's best interests in mind when acting on his or her behalf in financial matters.

The types of financial transactions the person holding a DPOA usually handles for a person may involve any or all of the following:

- Bills
- Banking
- Investments
- Real estate
- Taxes

KEY POINT

DPOAs can vary from state to state. It's imperative that you verify that your loved one's DPOA will be accepted in the state(s) in which it will be used if you don't employ an attorney to do so.

DPOAs come in two forms:

1. **Situational**—Only allows the DPOA agent to act on behalf of an individual when he or she is unable to—i.e., when a *situation* or scenario arises.

2. **Immediate**—Grants the DPOA agent instant authority.

DPOAs (either medical or financial) expire when the grantor dies.

Wrapping Up

Determine if your loved one has completed comprehensive advance directives. If he or she has, keep a copy and ask if his or her wishes have changed. It's not uncommon for people to change their minds on certain issues after their family is raised or as they age. Keep in mind this is your loved one's opportunity to have his voice heard when he is unable to speak for himself—it is not yours to judge or decide.

Key Point

Legal experts will tell you that the number-one use of a Financial Durable Power of Attorney is for long-term care planning, especially when the grantor is attempting to qualify for Medicaid to pay for nursing home care. Below are some websites at which you can create and print a DPOA:

*   www.RocketLawyer.com/Power-of-Attorney
*   www.FindLaw.com/Power-Of-Attorney
*   www.LawDepot.com
*   www.LegacyWriter.com
*   www.formblitz.com

 If the person who will be in need of care has had any form of major surgery or been hospitalized, these documents are most likely already on file. Otherwise, you'll have to have a gentle but frank conversation.

Chapter 5's Family Care Plan includes a decision tree matrix that helps a person make a decision regarding who should be an advocate regarding legal matters. That decision matrix is also applicable here. Use the decision tree matrix tool in conjunction with the tools on the following pages to complete this chapter's Family Care Plan.

FAMILY CARE PLAN

If there are existing advance directives, review them for any changes or inaccuracies and amend them.   Yes   No

1. If there are no Advance Directives currently in place, for whom are the Health Care Advance Directives being completed? (Please Circle)

     Parent(s)   Both   Other: _____

    Did that person ask you to be his/her advocate?   Yes   No

2. If the answer above was NO, have you discussed it with this person?
                                                          Yes   No

    If the above response was "No," schedule the conversation.
        I will call (name)_____ on (date)_____ to discuss completing Healthcare Advance Directives so that I will know what to do if he is ever unable to speak for himself.

3. The individual who is completing the Healthcare Advance Directives resides in a state that acknowledges the documents in the booklet *Five Wishes*.
                                                          Yes   No

    - If "yes," order the book or download the forms from:
            http://www.agingwithdignity.org

FAMILY CARE PLAN

- If "no," go to your state's specific website and download the pertinent documents or contact an eldercare attorney of your choice.

    _____Complete forms myself and download forms

    _____Call an elder-care attorney (Before calling, please refer to Chapter 3's section on how to select an attorney.)

Documents completed and located at: _____

4. Is a living will/advance directive in place?   Yes   No

Does it include a Do Not Resuscitate (DNR) order?   Yes   No
These documents are located _____

- If there is no DNR, does the person want a DNR in place?
    Yes   No

    See steps 3 and 4 above on how to acquire these documents.

Documents completed and located at: _____

5. All Healthcare Advocacy forms have been notarized. Yes   No

Copies of all Living Will/Healthcare advocate documents have been given to:

_____

My copy is located: _____

6. Is there a Financial Durable Power of Attorney (DPOA)?

$\qquad\qquad\qquad\qquad\qquad\qquad\qquad$ Yes $\qquad$ No

- If there is an existing DPOA, review it for any changes or inaccuracies and amend it. $\qquad$ Yes $\qquad$ No
- If there is no DPOA currently in place, who does this need to be completed for? (Please Circle)

    Parent(s) $\qquad$ Both $\qquad$ Other: _____

7. Have you the individual(s) who will be appointed as a DPOA been asked if he/she is willing to handle this responsibility? $\qquad$ Yes $\qquad$ No

- If the above response was "no," schedule the conversation.
    I will call (name)_____ on (date)_____ to discuss whether he/she is willing to handle the responsibility that goes along with a DPOA.

8. Is an eldercare attorney needed in order to handle the amendment of any forms or the creation of the necessary documents? $\qquad$ Yes $\qquad$ No

- If yes, call an eldercare attorney (Refer to Chapter 3's section on how to select an attorney.)
- An appointment is scheduled with _____ on this date/time. _____

9. If I plan to complete these documents myself, I have made sure that the forms I have purchased and/or downloaded are state-specific.

                                                       Yes   No

- I purchased them from: _____
- These were downloaded from: _____
- These forms have been notarized and witnessed?

                                                       Yes   No

By: _____

Date: _____

Copies of the DPOA documents have been made and given to:

_____

My copy is located at: _____

CHAPTER 6:

PUTTING YOUR TRUST IN TRUSTS:
TRUSTS, LIVING WILLS, AND PROBATE COURT

In this chapter you will learn:

1. What a trust is
2. The benefits of having a trust
3. The difference between revocable and irrevocable trusts
4. The steps required to establishing and managing a trust

RUSS AND YVONNE

A Family Meeting

In light of her new diagnosis, Yvonne wondered if she should take the decision-making out of Russ's hands and name her son as her advocate and name Russ's daughter as Russ's second advocate. There was so much to discuss. She called a family meeting. "Family" meant Yvonne's children and their spouses along with Russ's two children and their spouses. She would host a cookout and place Russ and her son in charge of the grill. She didn't want the grandchildren in attendance, just the adults. This wasn't a problem since all the grandchildren were in high school or college.

Just thinking about this type of conversation made Yvonne break out in a cold sweat—and break down in tears. But she could no longer carry the burden of covering for Russ's memory loss. More importantly, she was afraid. Not that Russ would be upset with her for sharing their secret, but that she would lose control of her destiny. She had made a personal vow after her mother's death that she and Russ would never become a burden to their children. Now it was time to review their estate, take inventory of their accumulated assets, and ensure that their finances would be protected and that they could remain independent as long as possible.

* * *

"Put not your trust into your money, but put your money in a trust."
–Oliver Wendell Holmes, Jr.
Supreme Court Associate Justice

In Chapter 1 of this book we discussed the importance of positioning your loved one's assets in order to qualify him or her for Medicaid assistance. In this chapter we will discuss in greater depth one of the most important legal and financial tools you can use to achieve this: a trust. The next few pages will explain what a trust is, its benefits, the different kinds available and which is the right choice for Medicaid planning. You'll be supplied with ample information on establishing a trust, whether you decide to hire an expert or do it yourself.

WHAT IS A TRUST?

The website www.law.com.com defines a trust as "a contract or entity that is created to hold assets for the benefit of certain persons or entities." A trust is in essence an intangible entity or series of legal documents established to easily transfer a person's assets/property upon death to family members, friends, businesses, or charities.

When we use the term in this book, we will be referring specifically to living trusts. A living trust simply means that the trust is created while the trust's grantor is still alive. (Testamentary trusts, on the other hand, are created in accordance with terms set out in a last will and testament and are effective only after the death of the trust's grantor.) A living trust is a must-have if your loved one wants to protect assets and incur minimal or no care costs (by qualifying for Medicaid) and avoid probate hassles that can arise after death. In order to take full advantage of a trust, the person who may require long-term care must have a solid understanding of its legal definition, purpose, and benefits.

Key Terms

The legal terms and jargon used in regard to trusts can be confusing, especially since some of these words are similar but couldn't be further apart in definition. The terms below will help you understand how an asset trust works.

Trustor/Grantor/Settlor/Donor/Creator

The trustor is the person who created the trust and/or who owns the assets that are to be placed within the trust. The trustor is also referred to as the grantor and sometimes the settler, donor, or creator. The grantor's role is to spell out the terms of the trust along with the conditions in which it will be conducted. The trustor may also serve as the trustee.

Trustee /Successor Trustee

The trustee(s) or the successor trustee(s) is the person (or people) in control of the decisions regarding the assets within the trust if the trustee is incapacitated or deceased.

Estate

The estate is assets/wealth that a person owns upon death. If a person has a living trust upon death and was the trustee, the assets are still his/hers and considered part of his/her estate.

Living Trust

A living trust is created during the lifetime of the grantor. If properly structured and funded, a living trust can be used to protect all the grantor's assets when he/she is attempting to qualify for Medicaid and enable a smooth transition from grantor to successor trustee upon the grantor's death. A living trust can bypass probate court so that property can go immediately to those the grantor/owner intended it to be allocated to.

Revocable Trust

A trust that can be amended by the trustor. The trustor can also revoke the trust. It is common for the trustor or grantor of the revocable trust to be the initial trustee/manager of the trust and a spouse or other close family member to be the successor trustee. Trustors also often list themselves as a beneficiary of the trust, with the spouse and family members named as contingent beneficiaries.

Irrevocable Trust

The trustor/grantor relinquishes complete control of the assets to a neutral and independent third party, who then becomes the trustee of the existing trust. The trustee manages the trust and its assets on behalf of the beneficiary(s) of the trust until the trustor/grantor dies. As a fiduciary in the relationship, the appointed trustee is required to exercise prudence in managing the trust.

ONE WAY →

The trustor/grantor and the trustee can be the same person. This is the decision-maker who controls the assets in the living trust. The successor trustee must be some entity other than the trustor/grantor. The successor trustee will control the trust if the original trustee dies or is unable to make decisions. It's disheartening when people pay to have a professional set up their living trust, only to find out later that it was only partially completed. After completing this chapter you will be able to avoid this situation.

CREATING YOUR LOVED ONE'S TRUST DOCUMENT

It is not necessary to hire an attorney to create a living trust, but it's a good idea if you want to be guaranteed a mistake-free document. If the person in need of care has significant wealth, consult an aggressive, expert eldercare attorney. (This is more than a do-it-yourselfer should handle.) If you decide to do it yourself, invest a little time in researching your options. There are many resources at your disposal and not all of them are created equal. Visit online bookstores or brick-and-mortar establishments like Amazon, Barnes & Noble, Office Depot, Office Max, or Staples. These stores will have books and generic computer software programs that are worth checking into. Another option is to visit stores like Best Buy, Costco, or Sam's for Quicken software packages. Quicken has both personal and professional versions of money management/financial planning software that in some cases also has legal templates for comprehensive advance directives, living trusts, and living wills.

- Use search engines like Google, MSN's Bing, and Yahoo.
- Check out Quicken.intuit.com, Legalzoom.com, Nolo.com, Livingtrusts.net, and Createmytrust.com.
- Check with your state's website for recommended forms; sometimes these downloads are free.

Whether you use an attorney or create a do-it-yourself trust using a software package, two things are essential:

1. The trust must be funded properly.
2. The trust document must be witnessed and notarized.

Many attorneys are generalists. They understand trust law on a broad level, but are not experts in the field. It is worth your time to seek out one who is. You'll find when you're "price shopping" for a good eldercare attorney that they don't come cheap. Depending on how much wealth the person in need of care has, the reduction of risk (depletion of assets to qualify for Medicaid) may be worth the legal costs.

An exceptional eldercare attorney also understands the tax ramifications of end-of-life planning, the family dynamics involved, and the nuances of Medicaid. These professionals will explain why and how to reallocate assets—not just to avoid probate court, but also in order to qualify for Medicaid, if desired.

Elements of a trust

The law requires three components for a trust. They are:

1. **Intention**—the rationale behind creating the trust must be clear (example: to protect assets; a charitable trust; estate planning/distribution).
2. **Subject matter**—Items held within the trust must be specified clearly.
3. **Beneficiaries/Objects**—Those who will benefit from the trust must be unambiguously identified.

Commonly Created Trusts and Their Purpose

Many types of trusts can be established. In order for the trust's creator to implement the proper trust, its imperative that the trust's owner be clear on both the purpose and the benefits it will provide.

Below, in no particular order, are some of the most standard types of trusts, the benefits they provide, which result in protecting intent of the trust:

1. **Privacy Trust**—Unlike a will, a trust is a private document, not a public record.
2. **Charitable Trusts**—Ensure that assets go to designated charities.
3. **Spendthrift Protection Trusts**—Protect beneficiaries who are unable to manage money, especially children or young adults.
4. **Tax Planning**—A trust lessens tax consequences. End-of-life financial issues become simpler and cleaner.
5. **Asset Protection**—Some people create a trust for the sole purpose of protecting their wealth or assets. This type of trust enables someone to dissociate himself on a personal level from his assets/wealth. The assets are owned by the trust and not personally by the individual.

KEY POINT

If a trust is not set up properly, its intent and the recipients' well-being could be at risk.

Funding Your Trust

In order to create a trust, the assets (financial/deeded and material) in need of protection are placed into the trust by the trustor.

For financial assets, like a checking or savings account, investment accounts, and even life-insurance accounts, when the owner dies, the recipient should not be an individual, but the trust.

You can do this by simply removing an individual's name from title work, bank signature cards or any other financial beneficiary line, and replacing it with the name of the trust (once it has been established). These assets now become the property of the trust. This is called "funding" a trust.

ONE WAY →

Living trusts are often established for asset protection. They reallocate or restructure ownership of goods or capital, and they have additional benefits, such as:

- Reducing estate taxes
- Providing protection and privacy
- Providing an inheritance for family members, non-family members, businesses, and charities
- Providing direction regarding financial wishes for minor children or adults in need of assistance

KEY POINT

All assets and title work either have beneficiary forms or transfer-of-ownership forms. If your asset is titled, you'll want to go to your state's Secretary of State website, which can help you with this transaction.

Example:

The name of the created trust entity is John and Mary Smith Family Trust.

> ***WRONG WAY:***
>
> ABC Insurance Company's Beneficiary Line: John Smith primary; Smith children equally proportioned secondary
>
> ***RIGHT WAY:***
>
> Beneficiary: John and Mary Smith Family Trust

Below is a suggested inventory list for a trust. Don't be afraid to contact the professionals who helped set up the investment accounts for help.

If a person's trust isn't properly funded, it has been created in vain, especially if he or she is considering qualifying for Medicaid to pay for care and has more than the allowable assets. If the objective is to avoid probate issues, all the grantor's property and assets must be in the trust.

Check off the investment when it has been moved into the living trust.

_____ Property

_____ Primary residence (For Medicaid, you may want to remove from trust. Consult your attorney.)

_____ Cottage/Cabin/Vacation Home

_____ Timeshare

_____ Rental or Investment Income Property

_____ Vehicles

_____ Automobiles

_____ Motorcycles

_____ RVs

_____ Boats

_____ Personal Watercrafts

_____ Bank accounts/Credit Unions

_____ Checking

_____ Savings

_____ Christmas Savings Funds

_____ Certificates of deposits

_____ Investments

_____ Employers Savings/Cafeteria Plans/Medical Reimbursement

_____ Life Insurance

_____ 401(k) or 403(b)

_____ Pensions

_____ Keoghs

_____ Mutual Funds

_____ Stocks

_____ Bonds

_____ U.S. Savings Bonds

_____ Government or Corporate Bonds

_____ Gold/Silver

_____ Livestock

_____ Futures

_____ Other (specify)

_____ Business Interests

_____ Corporate Shares

_____ LLS /LLC/LLP Shares

Revocable vs. Irrevocable Trusts

Once the intent of the trust has been determined, you or your loved one must decide whether the trust should be revocable or irrevocable.

The use of an irrevocable trust is the most trusted and legally approved method to provide relief for Medicaid eligibility because the assets are released only upon death of the trustor.

When an irrevocable trust is properly designed, funded and executed, it is acknowledged by the state's Department of Human Services as a suitable asset-protection technique for avoiding state-specific spend-down requirements in order to qualify for nursing home Medicaid financial assistance.

The use of an irrevocable trust, therefore, allows the grantor of the trust legally to benefit from the assets within the trust, even if the grantor can't access them. He or she will be able to qualify for Medicaid assistance while still preserving a financial inheritance for his or her loved ones.

1. Revocable trusts do not provide protection for one's assets or aid in Medicaid eligibility.
2. Irrevocable trusts do provide protection for one's assets and aid in Medicaid eligibility.

Choosing a Trustee or Trustees

For some people, the decision of whom to appoint to act as trustee (or successor trustee if the grantor will serve as the initial trustee) is more difficult than creating the trust. After all, your loved one must trust this person to honor his wishes. In a perfect world, the trustor's spouse or other close family member would be the designee. But what if there is no spouse or close family member to turn to?

Before appointing an individual as trustee, your loved one should take the following characteristics into consideration. This is a critical decision regarding the distribution of the assets that will be placed within the trust. The trustee should be level-headed, honest, and willing to assume the duties of administering the trust on a moment's notice. Remind your loved one not to let friendship or family relationships affect this business decision. This may be personal, but the financial aspect of this requires attention to detail.

The decision matrix below should help with finding the proper individual, even when hiring one is necessary.

TRUSTEE OR SUCCESSOR TRUSTEE DECISION MATRIX

Name of proposed Trustee:_____

Name of proposed Successor Trustee: _____

Is this person fiscally responsible?	Yes	No
Is this person able to think logically and react unemotionally?	Yes	No
Will this individual keep things confidential?	Yes	No
Will this individual view this responsibility as a burden?	Yes	No
Is this person's own life in order?	Yes	No
Is geography an issue?	Yes	No
Will this person keep your best interest in mind, and not theirs?	Yes	No
Do you trust this person?	Yes	No

If this person becomes ill or dies before you, who would be the successor trustee?

_____

Does the successor trustee meet the above criteria?   Yes   No

Once you have determined who you'd like to serve as your trustee, ask him or her. Be clear about the expectations and responsibilities that will be placed in his/her hands. If the person agrees to serve, move on to your successor trustee and make sure both people have original copies for their records.

If the individual declines, don't be resentful. He or she may just not feel comfortable or confident in their abilities to perform these duties or may simply not want any added responsibilities. If this happens, move on to the next candidate and don't let it ruin a relationship. That person is being honest; therefore their decision should be respected.

Where do you turn if you don't have family member or friend to appoint as a trustee? This scenario is not as uncommon as you might think. In today's world people often outlive their family or circle of friends and have no one who is willing to accept the responsibility of being a trustee. In this situation, seek out professional assistance. Fortunately, there are many resources from which to choose.

Perhaps the best method of finding a responsible trustee is to ask for referrals within your own professional network. You may also ask someone you trust who works with seniors or caregivers on a daily basis. Many people elect to hire a professional person whose sole job is to act as a trustee. (This is sometimes done even if the trustor has family options available.) Some smaller, locally based banks still have trust departments devoted to this specialty. Larger banks may offer this service, but will likely have minimum estate asset requirements. Also, some attorneys will act as trustees for their clients.

Below is a list of people who are usually informed and may be able to suggest a candidate or point you in the right direction to find one:

- Insurance agents
- Financial or estate planners
- Clergy
- Funeral-home employees
- Senior assisted living centers/nursing homes
- The local Council on Aging
- Senior wellness facilities
- Meals-on-Wheels volunteers or people who care for the homebound
- Attorneys

KEY POINT

Check references or the Better Business Bureau before engaging with a professional with whom you have no experience.

Reviewing a Trust

Once you've established a trust, it's easy to forget about it because it needs minimal upkeep. But trusts, just like wills and estate plans, ideally should be reviewed annually, or every two years at a minimum. Life changes often require changes in a trust.

If your life is not in transition, it's likely that nothing will need to be changed for many years. But when a marker moment occurs it becomes necessary to revisit—and possibly amend—the trust. Remember, a marker moment is defined as an experience in one's life that changes a person in some way.

Keep in mind that marker moments in life can happen to both the trustor/grantor and the trustee, and a marker moment can create a situation that warrants a change to your trust. Marker moments for the trustor or trustee could include:

- Marriage or remarriage
- Divorce
- Disability
- Death
- Depletion of grantor's assets
- Significant increase in grantor's net worth
- Grantor's change of mind regarding legacy
- Grantor's change of mind regarding appointed trustee

KEY POINT

If the trust is revocable, the trustee can be changed at any time with proper paperwork.

When the Trustor Dies

If the owner of the trust and the trustee die, it becomes the responsibility of the successor trustee to step in and act on behalf of the trustor/owner's wishes or intent.

When this happens, the successor trustee's role is to see that the intent of the trust is carried out, but not before any outstanding creditor debt, including funeral costs, of the deceased's is reconciled through the trust's assets. Typically, funeral homes are at the top of the list of creditors. If there is a surviving spouse, trust assets are not assessed estate taxes. Estate taxes are not assessed until both marriage partners are deceased.

A trustee should seek a probate/tax attorney to ensure all state/government requirements have been satisfied.

After the deceased's estate is reconciled with their creditors and taxes have been paid, it's considered to be in good standing. Now, the trustee can move forward with distributing assets to beneficiaries, be that an individual(s) or an entity. Once all the deceased's wealth and assets are distributed the trust is considered "dissolved".

Any assets that have not been placed into a trust prior to death will be taxed, and normal inheritance rules will apply.

FAMILY CARE PLAN

This worksheet will walk you through the process of establishing a trust.

1. Is a living trust document necessary in my situation?   Yes   No

   If yes, do I want to hire a professional?   Yes   No

2. Selecting an eldercare attorney:

   Ask a friend or relative if he or she has had to hire an eldercare attorney.
   Did they have a good experience?   Yes   No

   Would they use this person again?   Yes   No
   If not, why not? _____

3. Does this professional stipulate "eldercare" or "Medicaid" as an area of
   expertise?   Yes   No

4. Will this professional agree to a free one-hour consultation?
                                                                  Yes   No

5. Can this person confidently explain that they can reallocate a significant portion, if not all, assets so that a legacy can be left behind?

    Yes   No

    If yes—ask if this project is priced via an hourly fee or a package flat rate.

    If no—continue to seek out one who prices in this way. They are out there!

6. Select a Trustee and Successor Trustee

7. _____Notarize Trust—Once the trust is funded and completed it will have to be notarized. Many banks and credit unions, along with funeral homes, offer this as a free service. Check when this step is completed

8. Updating a Trust—Once the trust is created, keep accurate records of any amendments. Changes must be documented and the trust re-notarized.

CHAPTER 7:

HOW WILLS, TRUSTS, AND PROBATE WORK TOGETHER

In this chapter you will learn:
1. The differences between wills, trusts, and probate
2. How to save money by avoiding probate court
3. How to save money by minimizing estate taxes

RUSS AND YVONNE

Help From an Old Friend

Ever since Yvonne and Russ moved into their condo and Yvonne shared their medical diagnoses with their children, things had fallen into a comfortable groove. Yvonne was pleasantly surprised that the kids didn't hover, but did offer assistance regularly. Her biggest fear about letting the cat out of the bag was that everyone would start telling her what to do and forget that she had a mind of her own.

Too many times, Yvonne had watched her friends' children take over without considering their parents' wishes. They made decisions out of haste and convenience, not compassion. Somehow, the adult children's lives became more important then their parents'.

Russ and Yvonne had often commented on this selfish behavior and remarked that they wished they could remind those children that when their parents were raising them, it hadn't always been rosy. Their friends had willingly sacrificed so they could afford just the right jeans, the best vacations, and even cars for their children. It just wasn't right for those parents to be cast aside now. Russ and Yvonne never mentioned this to their friends, since it wasn't their place to say anything.

As the weeks moved on, Yvonne, with the help of her attorney, was able to secure last wills and testaments for herself and Russ. The only differences in the wills were that the personal belongings that each of them brought into the marriage stayed within each family. It was only fair to make sure each of their children had their family heirlooms. She was assured that probate would not be an issue when either of them died. Yvonne felt like she was making great progress in "legal housekeeping."

Yvonne hadn't been sleeping well lately. Russ often woke up in the middle of the night, disoriented. It wasn't uncommon for either of them to use the bathroom in the middle of the night. However, the other night, Yvonne thought she heard the water running. When she sat up, she realized Russ was urinating in a corner of the bedroom. It was over before she knew it, and Russ just carried on as if nothing happened. It was upsetting…and heartbreaking.

One day after lunch, Russ and Yvonne took a leisurely stroll around the block. When they returned home, Yvonne was exhausted. She desperately needed to take a short nap. She asked Russ if he wanted to catch a nap as well, but he said he wasn't tired. She asked him if he wanted to watch a movie. She figured that would occupy him for at least 90 minutes and she could snooze on the couch. Together they picked out a movie, and Yvonne was fast asleep before it even started.

She woke up to a blaring sound—the smoke detector. When she looked up, Russ was in the recliner, engrossed in the movie. Yvonne could see into the kitchen from the couch. Something was on the stove. When she got up to investigate, she didn't want to believe what she saw. On the burner of the stove was a plastic bowl with the remnants of what appeared to be popcorn.

Russ came in to see what Yvonne was looking at, and she tried to collect herself.

"Russ," she cried, "What were you thinking? You can't cook with a plastic bowl! You've made a huge mess, and now the place stinks!"

Russ looked at her and smiled. "What happened here?" he asked.

Yvonne melted. Russ just watched her with a glazed, far-away stare. Yvonne had known this day would come. She had read about the stage of dementia in which people get an idea, try to act on it, and then forget what they were doing, how to do it, or both! She surmised that Russ had been hungry. They usually had popcorn when they watched a movie, and he had thought he'd make it himself.

He had made a valiant effort. His memory of making popcorn must have reverted back to when it was made on the stovetop. That explained the bowl on the burner and the ripped-open microwave popcorn bag. This combined with the fact that Russ had turned on the burner and then forgotten it was a recipe for a potentially deadly outcome. Yvonne cleaned up the mess and found herself even more tired than when she had started.

Russ's oldest child and his family visited a few days later, wondering why they hadn't heard from Yvonne recently. After spending an hour with her, they were enlightened. Yvonne's breathing was more labored, and she looked exhausted. Russ was becoming more and more oblivious to his surroundings. He was starting to turn into a shell of the wonderful man they remembered. They helped Yvonne with laundry and made plans to go grocery shopping for her. They also offered to come and sit with Russ for an evening so that Yvonne could play bingo with the girls, something she loved to do and now missed.

Word had gotten around about Russ and Yvonne's declining health. Bob, their financial planner, stopped by unannounced one afternoon to have a heart-to-heart with Yvonne. He didn't feel it was right just to manage their wealth; he wanted to show them how to use some of the products he had sold them in the past. He needed to explain to Yvonne how she could benefit from the long-term care insurance they had purchased when they were in their 50s. Yvonne was surprised to see him on their front porch.

"May I come in?" Bob asked.

"Certainly, but we weren't expecting company, so the place is a mess!" Yvonne said as she tried to pick up miscellaneous items on the coffee table in the living room.

"I'm not here to be waited on or to give your house the white-glove treatment," Bob joked with her. More seriously, he continued, "I've come to remind you of something you may already know. I only want fifteen or twenty minutes of your time."

Yvonne gently guided Russ to the kitchen table and poured iced tea for everyone. Bob handed Yvonne an envelope. Inside was a copy of their long-term care policies, along with an up-to-date manual with customer service numbers.

Bob had highlighted items that were applicable to their situation. As Yvonne read it out loud, her voice started to crack with emotion. Their investment covered exactly what she needed. She could have kicked herself for not taking the time to investigate their coverage. She had assumed the policies covered only nursing-home care. But, in fact, their policies covered adult day care for 20 hours a week at a skilled adult day-care facility. Russ had no idea why she was crying and smiling, but he took her lead and celebrated too.

"Oh, Bob, thank you!" said Yvonne. "I didn't even think about adult day care, let alone consider that it might already be paid for. This can give me time to do things that have been neglected as well as let me rest and go to my doctor appointments without worrying about keeping Russ occupied! I'm so glad you came."

Before Bob left, he handed Yvonne a chart. It had all the customer service numbers for their different levels of coverage, the names and addresses of the preapproved skilled adult day-care centers in the area, and a list of exactly what

Medicare parts A, B, and C would pay for. It also outlined application procedures should either Russ or Yvonne require in-home care, which their policies also covered.

Bob mentioned that most people never take the time to understand what they have and many policies go unused. Likewise, coverage is often declined because policyholders don't follow the right protocols. He promised Yvonne that if she followed the directions and completed the proper paperwork, she would get help. She and Russ had made a very wise purchase.

After Bob left, Yvonne gave Russ a hug, and they sat down on the davenport together. For a moment, life felt good.

* * *

"Inheritance taxes are so high that the happiest mourner at a rich man's funeral is usually Uncle Sam."

–Olin Miller

In the last chapter we discussed the importance of establishing a trust. Now let's discuss the difference between a last will and testament and a living trust, along with the effect each might have on estate taxes and the probate system.

WHY YOUR LOVED ONE NEEDS MORE THAN A WILL

We've all heard Ben Franklin's adage that nothing is certain but death and taxes. But in the modern world, we've learned to blur the certainty of both of these.

Death is certainly unavoidable. Even so, we have developed cultural norms that help us control how we die. Living wills and Do Not Resuscitate documents provide legal instruments that prevent unwanted medical intervention; sedating drugs can help ease the physical pain of many long-term illnesses; and hospice provides emotional support and comfort to those dying, as well as to their loved ones.

Likewise, we can't entirely avoid taxes. Still, we can utilize legal tools to minimize the amount of taxes we pay. This chapter is devoted to understanding the financial impact our death will have on our loved ones and exploring in greater detail some of the financial tools available to help minimize the amount of taxes paid upon our death.

The Difference Between a Will and a Trust

A standard last will and testament is a document that lists the deceased's assets and stipulates how the assets should be distributed, under the authority of the probate court. A living trust is a legal tool that transfers a person's assets into a trust. After the grantor's death, a successor trustee will settle the estate in probate court so long as the trust is/was funded.

According to Consumer Reports, although most people are aware that they should have a will, almost 66 percent of Americans don't have one. (Truetrust.com)

KEY POINT

A trust never dies. It is an entity, not a person. It must be dissolved. A will expedites the probate court process; it does not eliminate it! The goal is to have probate court involved as little as possible with the distribution of assets. This reduces probate costs.

SAVING MONEY—AVOID PROBATE
What is Probate Court?

Probate is a protocol within our court system that was established to protect a family and its heirs, as well as creditors, upon the death of a family member. It was originally designed to keep the deceased's acquired wealth within the family as a legacy.

KEY POINT

Most people are unaware that probate court judges are envied by their judicial peers. Why? In some states, part, if not all, of their retirement is funded by the fees that are collected in probate court. Each time probate fees are paid to the court, a portion is directly contributed to a pooled retirement plan.

The word probate means "to prove." This is where a last will and testament or a trust comes into play. These documents are tools that prove what the deceased's assets were and how the deceased wished those assets to be allocated after his/her death.

When a person dies without a will, his estate is *intestate,* and state law determines how the decedent's assets will be distributed. If no will exists, the court is given the jurisdiction to appoint an entity to oversee all matters concerning the estate until it is considered dissolved or closed. When a person dies with a will, his estate is controlled by the will.

ONE WAY →

Probate court has nothing to do with taxes or property value. It has everything to do with ownership of property.

Probate sees to it that upon a person's death, all of his or her bills are paid and outstanding debt is settled. After all creditors are paid, probate will then legally transfer property to whomever it considers to be the next of kin.

In cases where there are minor children, probate court usually follows directives in the will in determining who is awarded guardianship of the children and will ensure that the children's financial interests are addressed.

Problems within probate court almost always begin with family. In many families a battle begins when a person dies without a will or trust. This is especially true in today's world of blended families and single parents. Conflict also often occurs between blood and legally adopted siblings.

If a person dies without a will, probate laws/court determine who the successor or heir(s) should be. Sorting out who is the next of kin is not necessarily an easy or clear-cut task.

> **ONE WAY →**
>
> Anything that goes to probate court becomes public record that anyone can access. Sooner or later, each state's probate court records will all be available online. One of the primary reasons people place their items in a trust is to keep their personal financial/material affairs from becoming public record.

KEY POINT

All probate court fees are directly deducted from the estate prior to a settled distribution.

Probate courts at times can be backed up, and settlement is not a timely process. If a family member decides to contest the court's decision, weeks can turn into months, and it's not uncommon for months to turn into years before a settlement is reached. When this occurs, the real winners are usually the lawyers and the court itself, which gets the processing fees—not the next of kin, who often discover the estate's worth is whittled away before any settlement is reached.

According to historical records, Presidents Abraham Lincoln, Andrew Johnson, Ulysses S. Grant, and James Garfield all died intestate. Each of these president's assets were probated, setting the precedent that no one is exempt from probate court if the proper documents are not in place.

Saving Money—Don't Pay Too Much in Taxes
What Are Estate Taxes?

The beneficiary (or beneficiaries) of the estate must also deal with estate taxes on assets they inherit.

KEY POINT

Legaldictionary.com defines estate taxes as:"...a federal tax on the transfer of a dead person's assets to his heirs and beneficiaries. Although a transfer tax, it is based on the amount in the decedent's estate (including distribution from a trust at the death), and can include insurance proceeds."

The Obama administration has determined that people who die between 2010 and 2012 with an estate that is valued under $5 million and pass the estate to someone other than the surviving spouse are not subject to estate tax. The surviving spouse has no limit and between 2010 and 2012 will not be subject to estate tax.

What Can Be Deducted from a Gross Estate?

Regarding federal estate taxes, the Internal Revenue Service (IRS) has determined that the following items can be deducted from the gross estate, thereby arriving at a taxable estate:

- Decedent's funeral expenses
- Administrative expenses associated with settling the estate
- Claims or outstanding bills of the decedent
- Certain charitable contributions
- Certain items of property left to the surviving spouse
- Estate taxes paid to state in which the decedent was living, or to the District of Columbia
- Property that is passed to the surviving spouse or by means of a trust (this is the most important deduction)

ONE WAY

Federal tax is eliminated only if the spouse is a U.S. citizen. However, if the surviving spouse is not a U.S, citizen there are ways around this. A good estate-planning attorney can create a "Qualified Domestic Trust" that will enable a non-qualified spouse to obtain this type of deduction.

Inheritance Tax vs. Estate Tax: What's the Difference?

In broad terms, an inheritance tax is a tax that is imposed the beneficiary(s) who received any form of property from the deceased. The tax is not flat; it is calculated separately for each beneficiary. Each beneficiary is responsible for payment of his or her own inheritance tax. Another difference between estate tax and inheritance taxes is that inheritance taxes are assessed only by states, while estate taxes are assessed by the federal government and some states.

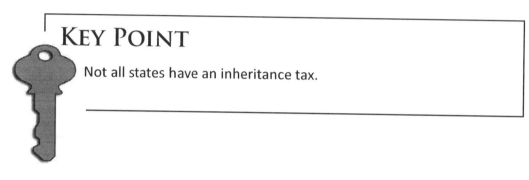

KEY POINT

Not all states have an inheritance tax.

An estate tax is imposed on the entire estate itself, not just on individual items within an estate (as the inheritance tax is). The federal government determines the imposed federal estate tax for all U.S. citizens. As mentioned previously, between 2010-2012, each estate will have $5 million that is exempt from federal taxation. The estate's executor is responsible for completing the federal estate tax return as well as the state estate tax return, if any.

ONE WAY

In states that do impose an inheritance tax, it's not uncommon for the surviving spouse or the deceased's children to be taxed at a lower rate than the other heirs.

KEY POINT

Not all states have an estate tax.

To get the most out of this chapter, complete the following Family Care Plan to make sure all the necessary legal and financial documents are in order for the loved one in your care. This will not be fun. But it is a necessary and responsible step that will save untold stress and financial headaches when death eventually occurs.

ONE WAY →

Most middle-class Americans will not owe a federal estate tax, due to the $5 million standard exemption for 2010-2012.

The plan is designed for anyone who is in the position of acting as an executor or personal administrator of an estate. It cannot be stressed enough that the prudent and responsible action is to prevent or minimize time spent in probate court.

If after reading this you are still feeling uncertain about proceeding with this task yourself, you can save money by locating all the documents listed below and compiling them into one file before visiting an estate-planning attorney. The more thorough you are, the less you will have to pay someone else to do.

If you were appointed as the executor or are the spouse of the deceased and you do not want the responsibility of administrating the estate, you can opt out. This is called a renunciation. You must submit a notarized letter to the court.

FAMILY CARE PLAN

This is not a legal template but a generalized guideline to use as you begin to navigate through probate court. Each state and county has different probate procedures. Check with the county (or countries) in which the deceased resided or owned property for rules, recommendations, and fees.

Step 1

Locate the deceased's important documents. These include:

_____A certified death certificate (has a raised seal)

_____The original copy of the most recent last will and testament

_____Revocable and/or irrevocable trust documents

_____All bank or credit union accounts

    ___ Checking

    ___ Savings

    ___ Money Market

    ___ Christmas Clubs

_____All investment accounts

    ___ Certificates of deposit

    ___ Stocks

    ___ U.S. Savings bonds

    ___ Mutual Funds

    ___ 401(k)

    ___ Keoghs

    ___ IRAs

    ___ Pensions

    ___ Annuities

    ___ Life insurance

_____All titled property
- _____ Real Estate
- _____ Automobiles
- _____ Watercrafts
- _____ Recreational vehicles
- _____ Farm equipment

_____All business or corporate interests
- _____ Limited liability Corporations
- _____ Partnerships

_____3-5 years of individual tax returns

_____All bills /debt and liabilities owed

Step 2

Enter the estate into probate or have your attorney initiate this process. Each court may differ slightly in cost and protocol. Entering probate can include, but is not limited to:

_____Petitioning for probate administration
_____Taking an oath to accept responsibility as executor/administrator
_____Making payment or petitioning to waive bond as executor
_____Gathering all consents and/or waivers from all parties involved
_____Requesting that the last will and testament (if any) be accepted by the court
_____Requesting authority from court to execute estate (Letter of Administration is the legal term)

The executor should open a separate bank account to eliminate any possible commingling of funds and to create a paper trail. This will eliminate headaches and chance of sibling suggesting that they did not receive their fair share. The probate process if everything is completed and handled properly, typically takes between two weeks and 30 days.

Step 3

Obtain a taxpayer identification number. You can do this at the IRS website (www.irs.gov). This number and a copy of the deceased's death certificate must be provided to financial institutions in order for the estate to be settled. For federal and state tax purposes it is wise to have an inventory of non-taxable items with an estimate of value.

Step 4

Assets must be appraised. You may want to hire an appraiser.

Assets in need of appraisal may include, but are not limited to:

- ____ Business interests
- ____ Titled assets
- ____ Real estate
- ____ Automobiles
- ____ Watercrafts
- ____ Recreational vehicles
- ____ Farm equipment
- ____ Personal effects
- ____ Jewelry
- ____ Artwork
- ____ Collections and collectibles

Step 5

Pay the deceased's bills along with any ongoing expenses until the estate is closed.

- ____ Funeral bill, if unpaid
- ____ Utilities
- ____ Mortgages
- ____ Personal loans
- ____ Legal fees
- ____ Taxes
- ____ Insurance (home, cars, etc.)
- ____ Doctor, dentist, and other healthcare professionals
- ____ Pet care/veterinarians

Step 6

Pay deceased's estate taxes, and all federal, state, and city income taxes for the year in which death took place.

The IRS website is explicit about what to do when filing for a deceased individual. If you don't handle your own taxes or you are not comfortable filing on behalf of the deceased, hire someone to do this. All professional tax preparers are familiar with what is required. Today, many people use tax software packages. Most of these federal and state software programs will interview the preparer. If you respond "yes" regarding filing on behalf of a deceased, the proper forms will appear, along with a tutorial to guide you.

Step 7

The final step is settling the estate with the designated beneficiaries.

Once all the estate taxes, income taxes, and outstanding debts have been paid (with proof of payments), the beneficiaries can inherit what was designated to them. Have each beneficiary sign a receipt upon settlement to avoid confusion and to provide the executor with solid documentation.

CHAPTER 8:

FUNDING IN-HOME CARE

In this chapter you will learn:

1. How to recognize when it's no longer safe for your parents to live at home
2. How to use Medicare
3. How to find free money

RUSS AND YVONNE

A Turn for the Worse

It was Yvonne's birthday, and her oldest child and his wife wanted to take her to her favorite restaurant for lunch. They had made arrangements for Russ to be at adult day care. Yvonne had been looking forward to this for the past week. Before Russ's illness, he had always sent Yvonne yellow roses on her birthday. When his memory started slipping, she would send herself the birthday roses with a card reading, "Happy birthday, Kid." When the flowers arrived, she would make a fuss, give Russ a kiss, and thank him. He would believe that he had sent his wife flowers, and on some odd level this worked for everyone.

While they were at lunch, Yvonne felt her chest tighten. She didn't mention anything—just took a deep breath and tried to relax. This went on for about 45 minutes. Yvonne chalked it up to the emphysema. She was determined to enjoy her time at her favorite restaurant with her son.

When it was time to leave, she stood up. The look of panic on her face said it all. Yvonne couldn't breathe. The more she tried to catch her breath, the more anxious she became, until she finally collapsed. The next thing she remembered was being taken away in an ambulance. While the paramedics were tending to her, she kept trying to tell them about Russ. Her daughter-in-law was one step ahead of her and was already on her way to the adult day-care facility. Yvonne's son stayed with her. When things settled down at the hospital, the news wasn't what they had hoped it would be.

This had happened before, but Yvonne hadn't told any of the kids. She admitted that whenever her chest had felt tight or she blacked out for a minute she had attributed it to stress or her emphysema. What she didn't count on hearing was that each time she had blacked out, she had been having a mini-stroke, or transient ischemic attack (TIA). These are warning signs that a stroke may happen in the future.

From the looks of her x-ray, Yvonne had had many TIAs. The doctor said that if she didn't do something to reduce or manage her stress, she could die before Russ. For all intents and purposes, she was a ticking time bomb.

To add insult to injury, she now had to go on oxygen full time. The doctor admitted Yvonne to the hospital for observation. This left no one to care for Russ. The family realized this was a serious situation. They would have to make some delicate decisions and have some difficult conversations.

Meanwhile, one of the children needed to take care of Russ. Yvonne kept insisting he could stay at the hospital with her if they would just bring him a cot. Surely the staff would understand. But Yvonne's doctor wouldn't sign off on this. This was exactly the reason her health was declining, he warned, and he told her she needed to take care of herself and gain strength. Taking care of others wasn't the prescription.

The children called another family meeting while Yvonne was in the hospital. They figured they had a captive audience, and if she wouldn't discuss things openly, they could go searching for the documents they needed while she was still hospitalized. The children wanted to explore options and discuss what needed to be done in case their parents were unable to speak for themselves.

When everyone came into Yvonne's room after dinner, she knew what they were planning. She saw no reason to protest. Their intentions were good. Besides, she would have done the same thing. The good news was that they had no idea how well Yvonne and Russ had planned for this chapter in life. After everyone made small talk, Yvonne took over.

Much to her children's surprise, she was able to tell them the exact location of all their important documents, including the information that Bob, the financial planner, had brought over. This was a huge relief for the kids. However, it was only one of the topics up for discussion. When Yvonne thought the conversation was over, the children knew it was time to discuss the elephant in the room that nobody was talking about—Russ's care.

The time had come for two things: around-the-clock care for Russ, either in or out of the home, and in-home skilled care for Yvonne three times a week. Yvonne heard this but she did not listen. The family finished talking for the night but the discussion was far from over.

* * *

"Old age: First you forget names, then you forget faces,
then you forget to pull your zipper up,
then you forget to pull your zipper down!"

–Leo Rosenberg

I f you find yourself in the role of caregiver for an aged parent or loved one, you may recognize the truth in the above statement. You may also know a little humor can go a long way.

WHAT EVERY CAREGIVER SHOULD KNOW

The phrase "taking care of your parents" is a very broad one. It can range from checking in on them daily to moving them to a nursing home. There are no hard-and-fast rules about caregiving. Some adult children elect to move their parents in with their family and incorporate them into their daily routine for as long as possible. It's not uncommon for adult children to do the opposite—move into their parents' home while providing care.

There are also seniors whose adult children are unable physically to care for them and seniors who refuse to allow their children to change their own lifestyles to meet their needs. We've all heard it: "I don't want to be a burden to my family." But that argument is muddied when your aging parent or loved one is no longer capable of living alone safely.

KEY POINT

One of the biggest telltale signs that your aging parent needs help is a change in the home environment.

When the red flag warnings begin, it's time to act. All the previous chapters about wills, trusts, insurance, and probate will now come into play. If you haven't already done so, complete the family care plans at the end of each of those chapters because now it will all come together.

Knowing When It's Time to Make a Change

Each family's situation is unique. The common denominator is a defining moment when there is no longer any question that it is time to find a more permanent care arrangement for a loved one. This moment is sobering.

Just remember that eldercare comes in many forms, and, sadly, it all ends with the same result—death. Intellectually, we all understand the stark reality that a parent or respected and loved elder will probably precede us in death. Emotionally, most of us fail to prepare for it.

As the adult-child caregiver, you now have permission to take control of the situation, albeit gently. When your loved one is in harm's way and no one is able to provide care, you must seek a suitable solution. The tricky part is to find an affordable solution.

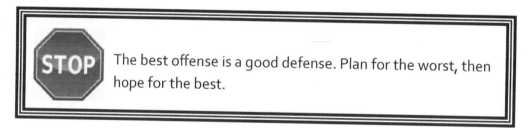

The best offense is a good defense. Plan for the worst, then hope for the best.

What does planning ahead cost you?
- Time
- A minimal amount of money

What does not planning ahead cost you?
- Unnecessary stress
- A significant amount of money

When planning for care, don't forget the obvious—in-home care. Today, it is not uncommon for an individual to be cared for until death in his or her own home. In fact, this has become a focus of hospice, along with allowing people to die peacefully when they no longer want extreme medical intervention.

USING MEDICARE

How to Pay for Care

In years past, many hardworking people retired and found themselves on a fixed budget. But they weren't worried. They had invested, planned and even saved for this day, with the expectation that their investments and pensions would be enough for them to live out their lives, and all would be well.

Fast-forward to today's economy. Blue-chip stocks have consistently shown a loss, pensions have all but disappeared, and the values of IRAs, mutual funds, and real estate have decreased. Even if they wanted to pay for their care, most of today's retired seniors would not be able to. It's not uncommon now for people (retired or not) not to have enough cash to cover their day-to-day expenses, let alone cover long-term care for a loved one. How does a caregiver resolve this financial dilemma?

Long-Term Care Insurance

Long-term care insurance was discussed in Chapter 2. If your loved one has long-term care insurance, your financial troubles may be solved, or at least minimized. It depends on what type of policy and coverage was purchased. If you choose to take care of your loved one at home, check to see if the policy covers in-home care. Most newer long-term care policies include in-home care, assisted living, and skilled nursing facilities. Long-term care insurance provides freedom of choice to make the decision that best suits everyone.

KEY POINT

If the person in need of care has long-term care insurance, don't forget to check for a caregiver benefit for in-home care.

How Medicare Will Help

If long-term care coverage wasn't purchased, you will need to seek financial help elsewhere. In **Chapter 3**, I introduced Medicare and Medicaid. Let's now dig deeper into these programs and learn how they may help pay for in-home care.

Medicare will not pay for long-term assisted-living care. It will pay for short-term stays when skilled care is required. Skilled care is given by a professional. Skilled care's areas of focus are:

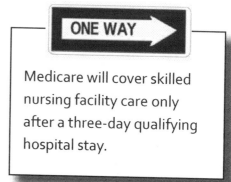

Medicare will cover skilled nursing facility care only after a three-day qualifying hospital stay.

- Physical therapy or rehab therapy
- Wound care sterile dressing
- Injections of certain types of narcotics

Medicare covers only care for specific skilled-care facilities for a limited period of time. "Limited" means short-term, or 100 days or less for each diagnosed medical need. Following are some examples of how this works, and the philosophy behind why Medicare approves certain procedures but not others:

Scenario 1

On January 4th, a Medicare patient's right knee is replaced. The patient is approved by Medicare to receive skilled care, based on the doctor's recommendation. Patient is preapproved for up to 100 days.

On August 1st, the same patient on Medicare has the left knee replaced. Again, the doctor feels that the patient needs skilled care in order to recover. The patient is preapproved for up to 100 days.

Scenario 2

On January 4th, a patient on Medicare will have both her right and left knee replaced at the same time. The doctor feels that the patient will be in need of skilled care and has the patient preapproved for 100 days initially, with an option to extend that period of time—not to exceed an additional X amount of days—if the patient isn't yet fully recovered. (X is based on the doctor's recommendation.) The patient is approved for skilled care in excess of 100 days until the patient fully recovers.

Which scenario makes more sense from a financial, medical, and recovery standpoint? If you said Scenario 2, you are correct. Any time a person receives anesthesia, there are risk factors. If a patient can undergo a single surgery, albeit an extensive one, he or she can recover faster.

Medicare (or any insurance company for that matter) would rather the insured have one long procedure and recovery instead of two separate surgeries, which doubles the expense and the patient's health risk. Medicare, just like any other provider, makes exceptions to their rules. The rules for health care are simply guidelines that are based on studies of others who have undergone those same surgeries. However, no two people are alike.

Medicare ultimately has the final decision, and following protocol is imperative. Nevertheless, it never hurts to appeal a decision. The worst that can happen is they say no.

Medicare wants to practice preventive care. Anytime they can place a patient out of harm's way and at the same time decrease their costs, they will. This is why paperwork and requests must be very specific. The more specific and complete the paperwork, the less confusion and stress for everyone involved: the physician's office, the skilled-care provider, the patient, and the patient's family.

 Call 1-800-MEDICARE (1-800-633-4227) or visit the "Ask Medicare" page at www.medicare.gov/caregivers.

Medigap Policies

Sometimes, Medicare supplement plans, or Medigap policies, provide long-term care coverage. You'll want to find out if Medigap (a Medicare supplement insurance, for example, Part B, etc.) was purchased.

If it was, read the fine print of the coverage to see if long-term care can be provided in the home, in an assisted living facility, or in a nursing home. If the answer is "yes," consider yourself fortunate. Most plans don't provide coverage for this type of care. Take note of stipulations and make sure you are in compliance so that there will be no questions about benefits.

LOW- OR NO-COST COVERAGE OPTIONS

Finding Free Money

What if your parent's Medicare coverage is exhausted and will no longer pay for care? Or if the type of long-term care needed is not in compliance with Medicare's rules? This situation is becoming common for Baby Boomers who are taking care of their parents. Often the caregiver's family rethinks their family daily routine and reviews their financial situation in order to accommodate their loved one.

When a family repositions and members take on new roles, it can cause an unplanned financial drain or hardship. A person's income could disappear entirely. It's imperative to seek out every possible solution.

Too often people assume there is nothing available. This simply is not the case. All it takes is a little bit of investigative work on the Internet, a few phone calls to government agencies, and time. Most eldercare programs are funded by our tax dollars. Look at it this way: your parents or loved ones have paid into government care programs their entire lives. It's now time for them to benefit from this investment. If they don't participate in the programs, someone else will. Look at them as entitlements, not handouts.

Where to Look for Programs, Funding, or Both

The tax-funded programs below are designed to be used for eldercare situations. They should get you off to a great start in your quest for care and assistance. Each state is unique. Programs, along with qualification requirements, will vary.

National Resource Center for Participant-Directed Services

Boston College piloted a program called "Cash and Counseling" in 15 states from 1998 through 2009. It provided payment for caregivers (with some restrictions). It was so successful that after the grant ended the states that piloted the program kept it in place.

In 2011, the Cash and Counseling program was available in the following states: Alabama, Arkansas, Florida, Illinois, Iowa, Kentucky, Michigan, Minnesota, New Jersey, New Mexico, Pennsylvania, Rhode Island, Vermont, Washington, and West Virginia.

This program varies slightly by state, and some states call it by a different name. In Arkansas it's called Independent Choices; in Florida, Consumer Direct Care Plus; and in New Mexico, Mi Via. Visit http://www.cashandcounseling.org/about/participating_states and http://www.payingforseniorcare.com/longtermcare/resources/cash-and-counseling-program.html for more information.

KEY POINT

Family caregivers provided the equivalent of $450 billion worth of care to their adult parents and other loved ones in 2009, an amount that makes caregivers one of the largest and most overlooked pillars of the U.S. healthcare system, according to a report by the AARP Public Policy Institute.

How to Qualify

In order to qualify for the Participant-Directed Services Program, the person in need of care must:

- Be interviewed by a Medicaid caseworker;
- Qualify for Medicaid; and
- Function as an employer and hire the caregiver, who will then receive compensation.

Checks and balances prevent abuse of the program. A caregiver is not allowed to receive, manage, or dispense the funds provided to the person in need of care. Another person must handle and allocate the funds in order to avoid a conflict of interest.

The Participant-Directed Services Program applies to in-home care only. It is not available to those in skilled care or assisted living situations, even if a third party (such as an adult child) is the primary caregiver.

Medicaid/Participant-Directed Services Asset Limits

As with any Medicaid program, applicants' resources are a major factor in eligibility. Resources might also be referred to as "assets" or "countable assets." State limits range from $1,000 to $8,000, but most are $2,000. There are many exceptions to what qualifies as a resource. For example, the Medicaid applicant's home can be a "non-countable" asset. Others are:

- Clothing, furniture, and jewelry
- One motor vehicle
- Prepaid irrevocable funeral plans
- Prepaid cemetery plots
- "Inaccessible" assets (such as...)

KEY POINT

Contact your state's Medicaid, social services, or Department of Human Services office for up-to-date information regarding the National Resource Center for Participant-Directed Services.

There are some additional requirements determined by states that must be met for homes to be counted exempt. The applicant must live in the home or intend to return to the home. The home must be in the same state in which the applicant is applying for Medicaid. His or her equity in the home must be valued at less than $500,000 unless the spouse resides there.

For couples, when one spouse requires care in a facility and the other is healthy enough to remain at home, the spouse living at home is known as the "community spouse" and is entitled to a certain amount of assets. The community spouse's assets consist of half of all the assets that are countable on the date when care begins. Not less than $21,912 and no more than $109,560. (This amount may be lower in some states and is subject to change.)

GET PROFESSIONAL HELP

Strategies can help seniors meet eligibility requirements; consult with Medicaid experts before applying. Case managers from your local Agency on Aging office may be able to help. Private geriatric care managers can help as well. Working with a Medicaid planner increases the chances of acceptance and ensures that your loved one preserves as much of his or her wealth as possible.

KEY POINT

If your loved one does not qualify for Medicaid, look into your state's or county's programs for seniors who have low or no income. There may be financial opportunities available for caregivers or people in need of care.

 www. GovBenefits.gov is the official benefits website of the U.S. government, with information on more than 1,000 benefit and assistance programs. You can get up-to-date, state-specific information.

FAMILY MEDICAL LEAVE ACT

The Family Medical Leave Act (FMLA) was put in place by the federal government in 1993 as a way to help employees protect their jobs and their benefit packages when they need to take extended time off from work to tend to a medical issue or to provide in-home care for a family member. (See Chapter 2 for more detailed information.)

Under the provisions of the Act, full-time employees can take up to 12 weeks of unpaid leave to act as caregivers. (The FMLA law has several restrictions; explore the law to determine whether or not you qualify.) If you are a caregiver who needs time more than money, this is the route you should follow. Check with your employer first, since not everyone's situation qualifies.

Seeking Grants

Explore grant programs when looking for caregiving options. Eldercare grants are a well-kept secret. With a grant, the caregiver has the best of both worlds. Depending on the type of grant awarded and its stipulations, the caregiver has revenue, which translates to freedom to care for the loved one without worrying about finances.

A grant is a program that provides money to qualified applicants that does not have to repaid.

Many seniors who may qualify for a grant are unaware of these kinds of programs. Grants are available for seniors from many venues. The Family Care Plan at the end of this chapter has more specifics on grant writing.

KEY POINT

The best thing about government grants is they are tax-free. Private-sector grants sometimes have strings attached. Federal grants are non-taxable and typically have no strings attached.

Some grant opportunities can be found at:

- Catalog of Federal Domestic Assistance (http://www.grants.gov/)
- Area Agency on Aging (http://www.n4a.org)
- The Administration on Aging (http://www.aoa.gov/AoARoot/Grants/index.aspx)
- American Association of Retired Persons (AARP) (www.aarp.org)
- State sites (http://www.usa.gov/Agencies/State_and_Territories.shtml, then click on your state to seek out what's available)
- The United Way (http://liveunited.org/)
- National Association of Area Agencies on Aging (http://www.n4a.org/resources-publications/readi-center/peer-consultants/resource-development)

Grants may provide funding for:

- Home renovations or modifications (to accommodate handicap accessibility, bathroom, and personal needs)
- Mortgage assistance
- Home health care
- Adult day care
- Caregiver respite
- Medical equipment
- Transportation
- Food/nutrition
- Rental housing

KEY POINT

The best place to find grant opportunities is on the Internet. Many times, when you contact a national agency directly, the person you speak to is unaware of what is happening on a national level.

When you apply for a grant, do your homework. The grant community takes some navigation. Since a grant is free money, the grantor controls the financial strings. The grantor can request specific information about the intent and results of the grant. Grants must be applied for via a written application.

Tips for Applying for a Grant

- Read the application directions carefully and provide all the required information.
- Start your proposal with a summary of your needs and plans.
- Stay in touch with granting organizations so that you'll know when funds are available.
- Make the proposal easy to read; include headings and a table of contents.
- Write short paragraphs that concisely express your needs and provide detailed plans to make your proposal easy to comprehend.
- Detail the overall and specific goals and how the grant will help you meet them.
- Include the short- and long-term objectives that the grant will help you attain.
- Include a budget that shows exactly how the funds will be used.
- Submit the proposal on time.

Source: http://seniors.lovetoknow.com/Grants_for_Senior_Citizens

The beauty of a grant is that it's free money; the downside is that the devil is in the details. Below is a guideline to use when requesting a grant:

Seek out available funding via eldercare foundations, organizations, and philanthropic groups; use the web and use specific key words in your search. Here are some examples of key phrases when searching Google, MSN, or Yahoo:

- Free money for seniors
- Grants for senior care
- Grants for long-term senior care in the home
- Grants for medical equipment for seniors

Research the group or organization that is offering the funding so that you can appeal to its mission statement and core values.

Begin with an executive summary. Always use "the three Ps:" **Purpose, Process, Payoff**. The executive summary should be only a few paragraphs.

For example:

"This grant is being requested for the ***purpose*** of _____."

"Here is a detailed explanation of the ***process*** that will be used for _____

_____

_____."

"The ***payoff*** for awarding this grant will be _____."

The next section is the narrative. Explain what you are proposing and how it will work. Be specific. Use **SMART** goals:

S: Specific

M: Measurable

A: Achievable

R: Relevant

T: Time-bound

- Create a budget showing all anticipated expenditures.
- Create a timeline and checklist of the "who, what, when, and where" the grant will involve.
- Establish a way to measure the outcomes of the project and explain how it will be modified for continuous improvement.
- Be persuasive. You must convince the grantor that this money will make a difference.
- Be neat and have someone proofread the document.

Grant writing isn't easy, but the rewards can be large. Don't be offended if your application isn't accepted. Ask for feedback to find out why your proposal wasn't funded. Learn for next time. You have everything to gain and nothing to lose.

KEY POINT

Watch out for con artists or Internet scams. Just because a company has a website and may appear credible online, it could be rip-off. Check out the agency's credentials. Don't pay money upfront. Use your common sense. Not all companies are bad; however, all it takes is one time and a person can be swindled. Remember the old adage, "If it's too good to be true, it probably isn't."

If you skipped over Chapter 3, 4, or 6, now is the time to revisit them. Their purpose was to prepare you for the financial how-to's and to know what your parents have in order to qualify for Medicaid. Chapter 3 focuses on actually qualifying for Medicaid. Its Family Care Plan, if completed, will serve as a guide.

ADDITIONAL TYPES OF ASSISTANCE

I've listed only some of the financial, physical, and even emotional assistance programs available. There are funds and programs out there; the key is knowing where to uncover them. Many community businesses, churches, and volunteer organizations offer assistance that is not covered by Medicare but that may be necessary for rehabilitation. These services may include:

- Meals
- Transportation
- In-home worship, blessings, and communion
- Grocery shopping
- Prescription refills
- Light housework
- Companion visits to doctors, dentists, etc.
- Pet care
- Bill-paying

KEY POINT

It's not uncommon for assistance programs to be free, since most are volunteer-based or paid for by the county. Check with your county's senior services website or the local council on aging.

FAMILY CARE PLAN

KEY POINT

Each state has its own rules, so check your coverage options in this order:

Private insurance

Medicare parts A and B

Medicare parts C and D

Federal programs

State programs

County programs

Grants

Fill in the blanks or circle the appropriate answer to the questions below.

Care funding options for: _____

(Name of person in need of care)

Person researching options: _____

(Name of person conducting discovery)

- I am the caregiver for the above listed individual.   Yes   No

- Relation to person in need of care: _____

- I have durable power of attorney for the person needing care:

                                                            Yes   No

FAMILY CARE PLAN

Step 1:

1. Does the person in need of care have long-term care insurance?

   Yes   No

   If yes, with what company? _____

   Do you have information about what is covered?   Yes   No

2. Is there a customer service number?   Yes   No

   If yes, number: _____

3. If there is no policy available, I called the customer service number and requested a copy of coverage.   Yes   No

4. Is the long-term care policy still in force?   Yes   No

5. Does this policy cover in-home care?   Yes   No

6. Does this policy have a deductible?   Yes   No

   If yes how much is the deductible? _____

7. Does this policy have a maximum amount of days for in-home care?

   Yes   No

   If yes, how many days? _____

8. Does care have to be skilled care?   Yes   No

FAMILY CARE PLAN

Step 2:

Start here if your loved one does not have long-term care insurance.

You'll need your loved one's Medicare card.

Name on Medicare card _____

Medicare policy number _____

1. Is your loved one in need of care for less than 100 days?

                                                                      Yes   No

2. Will it be necessary to have care after 100 days?   Yes   No

3. What is the estimated time care will be needed? _____

4. Can care be done in the home?   Yes   No

5. Does care need to be skilled?   Yes   No

6. Does the person in need of care participate in Medicare Part C?

                                                                       Yes   No

7. Does the person in need of care purchase Medicare Part D?

                                                                      Yes   No

NOTE: Call 1-800-MEDICARE (1 800 633-4227) or visit the "Ask Medicare" website at www.medicare.gov/caregivers.

8. How will the caregiver be paid if not through long-term care insurance or Medicare?

    Private Pay   Medicaid   Participant-Directed Services

    Grant   Friends   Volunteer Organization

9. If skilled care isn't necessary, who will be providing care?

   Family member   Volunteer Organization

   Friend   Hired help

10. Who will be managing and communicating with the caregiver regarding progress daily? _____

11. What primary concerns do you have regarding hiring a caregiver?

NOTE:

If the caregiver you are considering is not a family member,
ask for three references and call them.

1. Name: _____
   Telephone: _____
   How long did they provide care? _____

2. Name: _____
   Telephone: _____
   How long did they provide care? _____

3. Name: _____
   Telephone: _____
   How long did they provide care? _____

Questions to ask when checking out a reference:

Who did (name) provide care for? _____

How long was care provided? _____

What type of care did the caregiver provide? _____

_____

Were you satisfied with the care received? Yes   No

Would you use this person again? Yes   No

Is there anything else I should be aware of if I hire this person as a caregiver?

_____

Step 3

If long-term care is necessary and will not be funded privately or by a volunteer organization, seek out other financial avenues.

NOTE:

Whether programs are paid or volunteer, check references. If a program is church-based, ask around within the church. If it's a community volunteer-based program, ask the organization to provide references. Don't hesitate to ask. It's better to be safe than sorry when it comes to your loved one.

If you plan to use state, county, or local funding options for low-income recipients, you'll need the following:

1. ___ Past three months (or more) of bank account statements
   ___ Checking
   ___ Savings
   ___ Credit Union

2. ___ Income
   ___ Social Security
   ___ IRA
   ___ 401(k)
   ___ Investment Income
   ___ Pension/Retirement
   ___ Annuity
   ___ Keoghs
   ___ Alimony
   ___ Misc. income

3. ____ Past three months' expenses
   ____ Electric
   ____ Gas
   ____ Water
   ____ Waste management
   ____ Cable TV
   ____ Telephone
   ____ Rent or Mortgage
   ____ Credit card debt
   ____ Health insurance, Medicare parts C and D, and/or Medigap
   ____ Prescriptions
   ____ Outstanding debt (other than credit card debt)
   ____ Medical equipment rental
   ____ Laundry
   ____ Groceries
   ____ Life insurance
   ____ Pet care
   ____ Automobile
   ____ Gasoline
   ____ Car insurance
   ____ Bus pass/transportation
   ____ Other

If the caregiver is a spouse or sibling and is currently employed, he or she should look into his or her employer's FMLA policy.

_____Call company's human resource department

_____ Date of conversation

_____With whom did you speak?

Result: _____

Date to begin leave for care:_____

Anticipated return date: _____

CHAPTER 9:
CHOOSING THE RIGHT CARE FACILITY

In this chapter you will learn:
1. The types of care available
2. Ways to pay for a care facility
3. Tips for making the move

RUSS AND YVONNE

Yvonne to the Rescue

Yvonne had some setbacks in the hospital and became very frail. In fact, what was expected to be a week-long stay was turning into the better part of a month. Russ continued to live with his daughter and attend adult day care. However, he had lost all ability to carry on any form of intelligent conversation. He had to be told what to do and when to do it. He had stopped reading, playing, and even laughing. He spent most of his time staring blankly. He was rapidly declining.

Yvonne's lung capacity was very limited, and she required breathing treatments several times a day. She was on pure oxygen even when she slept. On top of everything else, she had picked up a virus in the hospital that knocked out whatever wind she had left in her. She hadn't walked any farther than from the bed to the bathroom in weeks. If she didn't regain muscle tone, she could fall and sustain further damage. Physical therapy was a must.

The kids took it upon themselves to tour assisted-living facilities and nursing homes. They found the information Bob had given Yvonne to be quite helpful. They learned the difference between private-pay facilities and skilled-care facilities. And they knew exactly when Medicare would stop paying for coverage and their parents would have to pay privately, use their long-term care policies, or qualify for Medicaid.

After visiting several facilities, they learned that there was no discrimination in care; whether a person was on Medicaid or private pay, the treatment was the same. They did notice a difference in facilities' cleanliness and the staff's attitudes. They noticed some big differences in activities and meals. All in all, the more they were involved, the easier it was to determine which facilities could be good fits for their parents.

Russ's dementia made his needs entirely different from Yvonne's. Although no one said it aloud, everyone knew that once Russ entered a facility, it would become his new home. He would not leave it until he died. Yvonne, on the other hand, needed very specific care. Once she was rehabilitated there was no reason, if she remained healthy, that she couldn't live independently.

Just as everyone had anticipated, the doctor soon told Yvonne that Medicare would no longer pay for rehabilitation. Yvonne's physician was not comfortable letting her live on her own. He suggested that he would discharge her if she arranged for skilled care in her home three times a week and placed Russ in the dementia unit of a reputable nursing home. If not, he would require her to transfer to an assisted-care facility. She was not surprised by this but didn't want to hear it.

She was now married to a man whose name was Russ, and who even looked like Russ, but was no longer Russ. The man she had married years ago had mentally left. On a rational level she knew that a nursing home was the right thing to do, but on an emotional level, she felt she would be letting him down. Sadly, Russ didn't know the difference. Daily, Yvonne would clean and feed Russ because it made her feel better. He seemed happy, although withdrawn and complacent. He smiled very rarely, and when he did, Yvonne always hoped it was because he somehow—from a smell, a sound or even just a movement—recognized her.

Yvonne moved home, and their investment in a long-term care policy paid off again. It covered the skilled care Yvonne needed. Russ was a different story. His long-term care policy paid for adult day care, skilled care, and a limited number of days in an accredited nursing home. This meant that Yvonne and the kids had to find other sources. Medicare would pay for 30 days of care, and the long-term care plan paid for an additional 90 days. After that, the family would need either to pay privately for Russ's care or qualify him for Medicaid.

This alarmed the kids. They had seen friends' parents go broke and even lose their homes in order to qualify for Medicaid. They were fearful and becoming short-tempered and angry.

Fortunately, Yvonne was way ahead of them. She had learned long ago that the government doesn't take anything away. When people do lose assets, it's due to fear and ignorance. Avoiding that fate was all about planning, and Yvonne and Russ had been prepared for this very day. Yvonne had learned from watching Aunt Carol take care of Grandma Ruby. She learned from both her mistakes and her good decisions. Russ and Yvonne's kids were about to learn the same life lessons.

Russ's caseworker sent Yvonne the Medicaid application. The kids figured completing the application would take at least a week. Yvonne could have completed the application herself, but she didn't want to be bothered. Instead she sent it to her attorney's office. After all, he had accurate records and documentation. His office had completed hundreds of these before. Yvonne and Russ's assets were already positioned for this very moment. After some forms had been filled out to make the trust funds irrevocable, Russ would financially qualify for Medicaid. It would take less than 30 days. Yes, their attorney would be paid a fee, but it was well worth it. No one was going broke.

The kids were amazed at how smoothly everything went. They were certain, based on what they'd heard about their friends' experiences, that this situation would be miserable. "Huh," Yvonne's son thought, "maybe I should have listened to her advice more often. One thing is for certain, when it comes to money, Mom knows how to save it. She always has."

* * *

Signs People Know You Are Aging

1. *No one expects you to run... anywhere*
2. *The things you buy don't wear out*
3. *People no longer view you as a hypochondriac*
4. *There's nothing left to learn the hard way*
5. *Your investment in health insurance finally pays off*
6. *You sing along with elevator music*
7. *Your secrets are safe with friends, because they can't remember them either*
8. *People call at 9 p.m. and ask, "Did I wake you?"*
9. *You quit trying to hold your stomach in no matter who comes in the room*
10. *You can live without sex, but not your glasses*

                              —Whittimer G. Willikers

Assisted living facilities come in all shapes and sizes. Some facilities are privately owned, some are corporate-owned, and some are state or federally owned. There is no one-size-fits-all facility. Choosing an extended care facility or even a permanent end-of-life residence for your parent or a loved one can be overwhelming. Unfortunately, the demand for quality eldercare facilities is currently greater than the supply. When this situation presents itself, the overall picture often turns into an economic one.

CHOOSING A CARE FACILITY

There are four primary ways people pay for assisted living or nursing home care.

- Private pay (cash)
- Long-term care insurance
- Medicaid
- Family and friends

Medicare does not pay for any assisted living facilities.

When someone rents or leases an apartment, it is for a specified amount of time. The contract states a beginning and an end, with an option to renew the lease. When someone enters into an assisted living facility, however, there is no end date. People move in because they are fragile. They will eventually leave, but there is no crystal ball that provides a date for that event. Most people who leave an assisted living facility do so as a result of:

- Illness or death
- The need to move to a nursing home
- A move to live with a family member
- The need to move to another facility due to finances

KEY POINT

The average stay nationally in an assisted living facility is 2.3 to 3 years before the resident moves from the facility for various reasons including health.

–National Council for Assisted Living, 1999 Study

Making the Move

Determine the type of care needed for this phase of your loved one's life, and make sure the facility you choose can provide that care.

Even though you may be looking for immediate care, it's best to think long-term when investigating facilities. In other words, can this facility take care of all of your loved one's needs under one roof, or within one campus? Will you have to move your loved one from facility to facility as his or her health continues to decline?

Shop around and seek referrals from others who have been in your shoes. If possible, bring your loved one with you when you tour the facilities. If this is not physically possible, take pictures or take the person on a virtual tour via the facility's website. Let him have a voice. If he is part of the decision process, he will be more accepting of the impending change. If this decision is jointly made, it will be a more pleasant transition for everyone.

People often think of this transition as a sad one. Why not view it with optimism? If your parent is moderately impaired or challenged, think of the freedom he and everyone else will gain. He will receive professional care in comfortable surroundings, and you will be able to be a part of his life without resenting the personal sacrifices you must make. If you choose the right facility, this can be a positive change for your family, as it has been for many families.

TYPES OF CARE

You'll need to know how to communicate your loved one's needs using the proper terms. There are three types of care:

1. Custodial
2. Skilled
3. Custodial and skilled

Custodial Care—

Helps a person with the day-to-day activities that are personal- or hygiene-related and aiding with certain noninvasive medical issues. Some examples of custodial care are:

- Bathing
- Dressing
- Toileting
- Helping to turn over
- Overseeing medications so that they are not forgotten
- Changing of wound or medical dressings

Skilled Care—

Requires a licensed and registered doctor or nurse on campus to oversee the care and medications the resident receives and to conduct any medical procedures that are within the scope of the facility providing care. Some examples of skilled care are:

- Injections
- Intravenous medications (IVs)
- Respiratory training
- Gastronomic tube feeding
- Catheterization

Combined Custodial and Skilled Care—

Just as it sounds, this option is a combination of both types of care. Although a person may begin his/her stay requiring only custodial care, in the end-of-life stages the resident may require skilled care in combination with the custodial care.

20 QUESTIONS

In order to determine what will work for everyone involved, consider the following 20 issues:

1. Is the person in need of care on board with this decision, or is durable power of attorney and/or guardianship paperwork necessary? One of these two must be in place in order for you to act on another's behalf and utilize any of their funding for such a move. **This is paramount!**

2. How will care be paid for?

3. What level of care will be necessary upon admittance—custodial, skilled, or both?

4. How does a caregiver organize their loved one's housekeeping, financial, medical, pet care, legal needs, etc.?

5. Who can explain the person in need of care's assets so the right financial decisions will be made?

6. Will the care facility's references check out positively?

7. What does the outside of the place look like?

8. Is the inside clean?

9. How does the place smell?

10. Can you arrive without an appointment to see firsthand the level of care and cleanliness at any given moment?

11. Are pets allowed?

12. How do others who live there look?

13. How do others who live there like the place?

14. How large are the rooms?

15. What are the meals like? (Ask to sample one).

ONE WAY →

Before you investigate anything, ask yourself if you have the legal authority to move this individual. Your intentions may be out of love and care. However, if the person in need if care is not participating, and you are doing this on his or her behalf, you'll need to have a durable power of attorney or obtain guardianship. Without one or both of these legal documents, it's a moot point.

16. Ask about the certifications of their staff.
17. Is transportation available?
18. How do they handle care transition as a patient digresses?
19. What type of activities do they have for residents?
20. How are they rated by the state? Look for complaints that are public record and can be found on the internet or by asking the facility to show you their ratings. Family feedback about these facilities are not hard to find—Google it, and you'll be sure to find reviews both positive and negative.

Most people who place their loved ones in care do so trusting that the facility will deliver what it promises. And most assisted living facilities and nursing homes do. Sadly, a few exceptions may give others a bad reputation.

If you are not comfortable with your findings at a facility, mark it off your list. Honestly, do you think the place will improve if it doesn't currently meet your standards? If you are uncomfortable now, it's a pretty clear sign that you'll be uncomfortable later. Save yourself unnecessary stress and angst, and trust your instincts.

 The Federal Trade Commission has a "Red Flags Rule" for reporting elder abuse. This regulation requires nursing homes to post their most recent survey ratings to the public. To learn more about this or how to file a complaint go to: http://www.ftc.gov/bcp/index.shtml.

Care Facilities and Financing

Read the fine print about finances and additional support and care. Many facilities offer special entry rates, much like an apartment lease. Rent, fees or costs of comfort items, like hair stylists, can be increased without notice. This makes budgeting difficult.

In the world of assisted living, cash is not king. There is no preferential treatment for those who pay with cash (private pay) over those who pay with Medicaid. This is a well-kept secret. Many nursing homes prefer Medicaid clients because they know their fees will be paid directly by the government into the facility's account. There is no question about when they will be paid. This makes budgeting beds and allocating resources significantly easier.

The idea that private pay care is better than Medicaid care is also a fallacy. Knowing that you (or one you hold dear) will not receive any better care in a facility as a private-pay patient than as a Medicaid patient may offer you some peace of mind.

Meeting Prescription Requirements

One of the biggest budget-busters when it comes to long-term care is prescription medications. Care facility residents often require prescriptions. When you choose an assisted living or nursing home, it is imperative that you are clear on the policy for administering and refilling medications. This often becomes a point of contention between management, staff, and the residents or residents' families.

Everyone is human, and mistakes can happen for a variety of reasons—staff turnover, unclear instructions, or accidental oversights. They can happen in care facilities, hospitals, and even in doctor's offices. Thankfully, they don't happen often.

Your main concern shouldn't focus on the distribution of medications, but rather on how the pharmaceuticals and their distribution are charged.

Charges rack up much in the way that hospital charges accrue. Some facilities will dispense only medications that are provided in accordance with specified requirements, such as bubble dispensers and blister packs. These dispensers can become expensive and many may only be filled through private or in-house pharmacies. Some facilities only send out for medications because there is no in-house or contracted licensed pharmacist.

- Your loved one's prescriptions can be filled at their own pharmacy, where the pharmacist is familiar with their medication needs and will check for medication compatibility.
- Your loved one can have prescriptions filled through health insurance and mailed in bulk to the care facility.

Ask the Tough Questions

Again, although many of these facilities have high standards and wonderful reputations, you should ask the hard questions. If there is nothing to hide, an admittance director or facility manager will be happy to answer all your questions. If something has occurred at their facility, this will give them the opportunity to share with you what new procedures have been instituted to prevent it from happening again.

When addressing a difficult topic, keep in mind the sensitive nature of the topic, and don't make accusations or speak in a threatening manner. Simply state that you have a few more questions that may be delicate but that you need answered for your peace of mind. Remember, you are your loved one's advocate.

Examples of tough questions are:

- How is the day staff different from the night staff?
- What types of background checks are done on your employees to ensure they have the necessary professional credentials?
- What security measures or protocols are in place to prevent solicitors, non-family members, and potential predators from having access to your loved one?
- Have your staff/employees been checked to ensure none are sexual predators?
- What types of measures are in place to ensure the distribution of proper medications?
- What is the protocol if a serious injury, illness, or death unexpectedly occurs?

KEY POINT

If you don't ask the tough questions, you'll never know the truth. Your parent took care of you as a child. He or she looked out for your safety and health and asked questions on your behalf. Now it's your turn!

At this stage, your role as a caregiver evolves. Tough decisions will affect you and your parent. This is uncharted territory, much like parenting the first time around. We learn from others who have walked in our shoes before us. The Family Care Plan on the following pages will help you with some of these decisions.

FAMILY CARE PLAN

To decide what type of care is necessary, talk to your loved one's physician.

_____ In-home

_____ Short-term

_____ Long-term

_____ Assisted living

_____ Nursing home

How will this be paid for?

_____ Long-term care insurance

_____ Private pay

_____ Medicaid

_____ Other(specify)? _____

1. Make a list of pros and cons of in-home care versus full-time care in a separate facility. This may provide clarity for you and your loved one.

PROS   CONS

FAMILY CARE PLAN

2. Ask your loved one these questions:

   - How will this new living arrangement make your life more comfortable?
   - Why is this decision better for your health?
   - Are there any concerns you have about this choice?
   - What amenities will you have there that you don't have now?
   - What are your fears?
   - What can I do to make this easier for you?
   - What can I change/bring to make your living accommodations more like home?

3. Is the person in need of care in agreement with you, or is durable power of attorney and/or guardianship paperwork necessary for you to act on his or her behalf and to use his or her funds?

4. Organize all your loved one's needs in the following categories:
   - _____ Housekeeping
   - _____ Medical
   - _____ Financial
   - _____ Personal
   - _____ Pet care
   - _____ Legal
   - _____ Funeral

APPENDIX:

FUNERAL PREPLANNING

In this chapter you will learn:
1. The benefits of planning a funeral
2. How to pay for a funeral
3. Alternatives to the traditional funeral

RUSS AND YVONNE

And Life Goes On

"Hey, Dad. How you doing?" Russ's oldest child asked while entering his room. "Looks like you haven't shaved in a few days. We'll have to talk to your attendant about that, unless you're going for the unshaven look! Come to think of it, I've never seen you with a mustache or a beard."

Russ was completely withdrawn and didn't talk. He didn't eat unless he was spoon-fed, and could only sit in his wheelchair and stare out the window. His once-fit body was bent, thin, and weak. He was clearly in the end stages of his disease. He'd lived in this care facility for almost five years. No one thought he would live this long. It's amazing what the human body can endure with a strong heart.

All of the children, both Russ's and Yvonne's, made it a point see Russ and check on his care weekly. This was the promise they made to Yvonne right before she died two years ago. While she was still living, Yvonne came to have lunch or dinner with Russ every day. Each time she came to see Russ; he turned his head and smiled in her direction. Regardless of what the facts or his physicians said, she was sure Russ knew her. She believed that until the day she died.

Yvonne died on their wedding anniversary—not from emphysema, ironically, but from a broken heart. They say when people are truly connected they start to look like each other and even act like each other. Although Yvonne had become stronger and learned how to manage with portable oxygen, she really missed being needed by and caring for Russ. Each time she visited him, a little bit of her heart died, and she became more depressed. Her appetite slowly declined, along with her enthusiasm. She slowly gave up bingo, bowling, golf, and her weekly night out with the girls. Her weight dropped from a healthy 142 pounds to 106. Her children were with her when she died.

Yvonne had planned for her death, just as she had planned in life. Her children said it was one of the best gifts of love she ever gave them. She had prepaid for both her own funeral and Russ's when they placed Russ in a nursing home.

Yvonne's funeral was small and practical, just like Yvonne. She had requested to be cremated since she didn't see any value in wasting all that money on a casket that she wouldn't appreciate anyway. Her children struggled with this because they wanted a traditional funeral. Their funeral director explained to them that even though Yvonne had left a guide for them to follow, they could still do things their way. They immediately said, "No!" They chose to honor her wishes; as she had taken care of them when she lived, she also took care of them in her death.

There were a few nuances to Yvonne's funeral plans that surprised the children, but they fulfilled her every wish. When Yvonne married Russ, she was a widow. Her first husband had died in an accident. Without him, she wouldn't have had her children. Therefore, she wanted a portion of her cremains to be buried on top of his grave. She also requested that her thumbprint be taken so each child could have a "thumbie"—a charm of her thumbprint. She had prepaid for that as well.

Russ, on the other hand, had made it very clear while he was of sound mind that he didn't want to be cremated. In many ways, he was an old-fashioned gentleman, and he wanted an old-fashioned funeral. His funeral wishes were entirely different from Yvonne's. The children promised Yvonne that they would follow his plans.

One of Russ's wishes was that if Yvonne died first, a portion of her cremains would to be placed with him in his casket. If she died after him, he asked that some of her cremains be buried on top of his grave just as part of them would be buried with her first husband. Yvonne had died first, but in a way, Russ had died years ago. Russ had attended Yvonne's funeral, but he had no idea where he was…or why.

Russ and Yvonne were not any different from their peers in terms of age, socioeconomic class, life experiences, or health issues. The difference was that Yvonne and Russ had the foresight to draw from their experiences, learn from their mistakes, listen to what others would have done differently, ask difficult questions, and plan for the future. They learned that if they asked for help, they would lovingly receive it. The legacy that Yvonne and Russ left to their children was more than a financial one. It was a legacy of love and personal responsibility.

* * *

"Life is not measured by the number of breaths you take, but by the moments that take your breath away."

—Anonymous

When a person decides to enter a care facility, the admissions coordinator will ask, "If death should occur while you are under our care, what funeral home would you like us to notify?" If that person is applying for Medicaid, the facility will also often ask for a copy of his or her prearranged funeral for its files. One of the reasons for devoting a chapter of this book to funeral planning, both pre-need and at-need, is the role it plays in asset allocation when an applicant wants to qualify for Medicaid.

Often people are afraid to discuss death and dying. If they are superstitious, they may fear jinxing themselves. These fears are unnecessary. Death is a part of life, and as with all things in life, it is best to be prepared for it.

PLANNING A FUNERAL

On the rare occasion that funeral planning is at the top of someone's to-do list, it is usually as a result of a crisis. Those who have prearranged and prefunded their funerals feel greatly relieved. In fact, most are surprised by how easy is. Prearranging your own funeral puts you in the driver's seat. There are no timelines, stresses, or finances to worry about. You have the gift of time to explore all options, including payment options. When a death occurs, families have all the same options, but their decision-making capabilities are often clouded by emotions. Additionally, and unfortunately, financial options also are often limited, placing an unexpected financial hardship on the family.

By prearranging and prefunding your funeral, you will be saving your loved ones the emotional and financial burden of doing it for you while they are grieving.

Benefits of Preplanning a Funeral

The benefits to prearranging and prefunding one's funeral far outweigh the reasons or excuses not to.

There are three primary reasons to preplan a funeral:

1. Those who are left behind have the comfort of knowing they provided the funeral their loved one wanted.

2. Everything can be paid for (with the exception of obituaries, flowers, clergy, opening and closing of the grave—basically anything that prices aren't controlled by the funeral home), sparing loved ones any financial burden.

3. Even if the funeral was not prepaid, the family will know the funeral selections were preplanned by the deceased and were within the deceased's financial means. This will eliminate overspending out of regret or guilt.

Funeral planning certainly won't take away the pain of loss, but will allow the survivors to focus on their emotional needs.

KEY POINT

Funeral plans can be changed at any time and should be completely transportable to another funeral home. If a funeral home does not offer these two provisions, find one that does.

Funeral Planning Has Medicaid Qualification Benefits

As mentioned earlier, prepaid funeral plans are considered exempt assets when applying for Medicaid. But as always, there are rules involved.

A well-kept secret within the law lets the Medicaid applicant:

1. Prepay for his own funeral
2. Prepay for his spouse's funeral
3. Prepay for his "blood" children's funerals
4. Prepay for his "blood" grandchildren's funerals

You may pay for all these and still be within compliance for Medicaid qualification. This is a common practice of those in the know. The catch is that prepaid funerals must be made irrevocable, which a knowledgeable funeral director or arranger can do.

All prepaid funeral plans can be transferred to any funeral home of the recipient's choice during their lifetime. Work only with a funeral home that honors transportable plans. The funeral contract, while transportable, cannot be cashed in until the recipient's death—hence the term "irrevocable."

How to Preplan a Funeral

Funeral planning is a two-step process:

Step 1

The first step is the most important one—sitting down with a funeral home professional and recording your biographical information and funeral preferences.

It is certainly possible to do most of this on your own, in your own home. But there are plenty of reasons why you shouldn't. While you may record your personal information, what type of funeral you want, and even write your own obituary and put that information in a safe place—maybe in a family Bible, a filing cabinet, or a safe deposit box—no one may know about it, or the person who knows may forget about it. Then, when you die, your preferences will die with you. This is especially true when there is no surviving spouse, and this situation can cause misunderstandings and hard feelings among your loved ones who are already under the stress of grieving.

Furthermore, by working with a funeral professional, you will be able to plan your funeral down to the last detail, including decisions regarding the casket or urn you want and whether you would like memorial brochures and in what design. Every choice you can make for yourself will spare your loved ones from having to choose once you are gone. And you will be able to choose items within your price range. Even if you don't prepay for your funeral, knowing your wishes will spare your loved ones from arguing over what they think you would have wanted as well as spare them any guilt about choosing a less-expensive item over one that's more expensive.

Step 2

The second step of funeral planning is deciding how to pay for it. In general, there are six ways people pay for a funeral.

- Life insurance
- Savings/investments
- Family/friends
- Prepayment through a funeral home
- Single Premium Final Expense Policies
- Totten Trusts

Let's explore each of these options in more detail.

1. Life Insurance

Traditionally, people purchased life insurance to take care of the living, or more precisely, the loved ones they left behind. Insurance was purchased to supplement the survivors' lifestyles once the deceased's income was no longer available. This was a way for parents to ensure their surviving dependent children would be taken care of financially.

Many times people purchase insurance and assume it will be in force when they die. This is not always true. Often a policy was a job benefit that ceased to be in effect when they retired. Or people purchase term insurance, which sometimes decreases in value over time and/or ceases to be in force after a certain age. The policy terminates, leaving them with no coverage at all. It's imperative that you check to see what type of insurance your loved one has.

Frequently, people have insurance policies with cash values. An experienced funeral planning professional will know how to make that cash value work toward prepayment of the funeral while still allowing you to keep the insurance policy intact until death occurs. This option is win-win because it makes the cash value of the policy disappear. Therefore, this insurance policy will not count against the individual as an asset if he or she has to seek Medicaid assistance for assisted living or a nursing home admission.

2. Savings/Investments

In the last year of a person's life, his or her entire life savings can be wiped out. It's too often the case that in the last six months of life, doctor visits, hospital stays, and prescription drugs—not to mention home-health care or assisted-living arrangements—erode a person's wealth so that by the time death occurs no money is left for the funeral, let alone to support the surviving spouse.

Any form of savings or investments will count as an asset for Medicaid assistance. So people either spend their savings on healthcare or spend it down on other things in order to qualify for Medicaid. As we've discussed in detail earlier, paying funeral expenses in advance is a good option when spending down is necessary.

3. Friends/Family

Although friends and family may sometimes be counted on to make funeral arrangements, this solution is often referred to as "a prayer and a promise" because there's no predicting the results. People do not take into consideration the emotional and financial burden that funeral planning places on their loved ones' shoulders. Conflict can arise when adult children want to spend more on a funeral than they can afford. Each family has debt and financial responsibilities, and questions about who can afford what may result in hard feelings. Moreover, not all family members may agree on the type of funeral to hold; questions regarding burial or cremation and religious preferences are often points of contention.

Today, family members often live in different communities. Unless neighbors have the names, addresses, or phone numbers of the adult children, it becomes difficult for the next of kin to be contacted to make decisions. To ensure you have the type of funeral you want, arrange it yourself.

4. Prepaid Funerals Through a Funeral Home

Most funeral homes offer preplanning and have a staff member who specializes in this area. The funeral industry is highly regulated regarding the funding or investment companies they can place funds with. Funeral homes are also regularly audited by the state to ensure that their pre-need funds are valid and invested properly and that there are written documents for each pre-funded funeral. Each state may have its own set of rules as to the amount a prepaid insurance contract can be written for. But regardless of the amount, if the prepaid funeral is made irrevocable, it will not count against an applicant applying for Medicaid.

5. Single Premium Final Expense Policies

These policies are very similar to option 4. The difference between the two is typically in the policy growth at the time of death for the funeral home and state regulations. (Some final expense policies will reflect a slight increase while others do not.) In some states, funeral homes can sell only prepaid funeral policies that are designed specifically for funeral homes (option 4). In others they can sell both. The difference between option 4—a prepaid funeral insurance contract—and option 5—a single premium final expense contract—is as follows:

With option 4 (prefunding a funeral) the person selects/designs a funeral at today's prices because he pays for it today. Thus, the funeral price is "guaranteed" by the funeral home or by state law.

Option 5 allows a family to set aside money in a final expense insurance contract that can be written by their trusted insurance advisor, attorney, financial planner—and in some states, their funeral home. However, the difference between option 4 and option 5 is that with option 5, the funeral cost is not guaranteed at today's prices. The policy simply remains in force until death, when it can be used by the deceased's survivors to select and pay for an appropriate funeral.

Regardless of whether the applicant's prepaid funeral is one written through a specially designed insurance policy for funeral homes (option 4) or a final expense policy (option 5), to qualify for Medicaid, the applicant must have a funeral home agree to:

- Accept assignment for payment
- Make it irrevocable
- Agree to provide a statement of goods and services, guaranteeing to provide the funeral and or components of the funeral for the face value of the insurance contract. (The insurance contract must be in force at the time of death or there is no guarantee.)

6. Totten Trust

Totten Trusts were created in the early 1900s. The name is after a 1903 court case by the name of Totten. They are funeral accounts that are payable on death. They allow a depositor to set aside money in a bank account or security to be used for the sole purpose of paying for his or her funeral. The institution that holds the funds must place them in a trust account and keep them secure until the depositor's death. Upon proof of death, those funds are released, passed through probate untaxed, and given to the entity providing the funeral. At one time, the Totten Trusts were considered irrevocable, and there was no access to those funds until death. Most states recognize these trusts, but not all. Today Totten Trusts are not all that common as they can be accessed by the depositor and even creditors of the depositors.

TAKING CONTROL OF YOUR FUNERAL

Funerals don't have to be expensive or even be held at a funeral home to be meaningful or relevant. Years ago, funerals were held in the deceased's home. Funerals are now hosted in funeral homes and churches, due to reasons including:

- Sanitary/health hazard issues if the body is present and has not been embalmed (especially after 24 hours if the deceased has not been held in refrigeration/cold storage)
- Parking
- Physical space
- Restrooms
- Technology
- Not wanting to deal with the emotions of remembering a funeral or visitation in one's living room
- Scheduling
- The number of people it takes to prepare the food, printed material and physical set up for a funeral
- Insurance liability if a guest accidentally injures themselves or if something should happen to the deceased
- Privacy: depending on the size of the location, there many be no place for the family and or clergy/celebrants/speakers to get away and regroup or prepare for the service

Over the past few years, Baby Boomers have experimented with hosting funerals in non-traditional locations. Examples of this would be VFW halls, country clubs, lodges, reception hall, and even community centers. This should come as no surprise because as the Baby Boomers continue to age, they continue to change the norms—even norms that were once considered reverent. Funerals are no exception. Hosting funerals outside of a funeral home or church is becoming more popular, but it isn't without its challenges. In fact, those who take this route often say that it was a lot of work and compare it to trying to host a wedding, complete with reception, without the ability to plan months ahead of time. In theory, it sounds very doable; in reality, it's physically and emotionally draining.

Yes, some elements still remain the same, including:

- The deceased
- A grieving family
- Financial constraints
- Merchandise—casket, vaults, urns, printed material, monuments, keepsakes
- Death certificates
- Obituaries

and often:

- Cemetery
- Reception
- Facilitator/Clergy/Celebrant

Now let's toss in the dynamic of external, unconventional factors that go hand-in-hand with boomer families:

- Geographical disparity
- Other obligations—work, school, sports, vacations, etc..
- Scheduling difficulties
- Wanting to have a parent cremated and keep the cremains with them in their home until the second parent dies, so they can have one joint funeral/burial event.
- Storing the first parent's cremains until the second parent dies
- Mixed ethnicities or religious beliefs (examples would be mixed faith marriages of the deceased or their family)

In years past, our society expected the ritual of a casketed burial and understood funerals were not meant to be convenient. In fact, much like childbirth in years past, inconvenience was a given!

Today, many people prefer cremation. Why? Some reasons include:

- Reluctance to have their body publically viewed
- Friends and family living far away; therefore, scheduling a funeral at a later date
- Few living friends and family
- Not wanting to be buried in the ground or mausoleum
- Wanting to be scattered
- Wanting to donate their body to science
- Not understanding the value for some form of a ritual or service that provides closure for those left behind so they can share grief and say goodbye
- Cost (although this can be a misconception depending on the type of memorial, funeral, or even a gathering

Cremation is not good or bad. It's a personal preference. In fact, there are many advantages to cremation such as:

- Mobility
- Convenience—providing the option of having a memorial, funeral, or gathering at some point in the future, where people can plan to attend ahead of time, much like a wedding.
- No burial costs

This list can go on, however, outside of the legalities, which a funeral home and/or a licensed director must perform, families can create heartfelt, relevant, and meaningful tributes on their own when their loved one is cremated. Today's computers, video capabilities, and software has enabled families to make personalized guest books and other printed and multimedia materials. Challenge yourself to think of the benefits of hands-on participation with funerals.

KEY POINT

Research has shown that people reap emotional and physical benefits by being involved in their own funeral planning (either before death or at the time of death).

Just a decade or so ago, most people with terminal or age-related illnesses died in hospitals. But that changed with the introduction of hospice care. Today, through the assistance of hospice, families are present through their loved one's illness from its onset until death. Hospice care can be in the home or in a home-like setting, which many people attest is a rewarding experience. Hospice can allow the person who is dying to have a voice in his or her tribute. Hospice encourages families to accept the experience as a positive circle-of-life experience.

Today's Baby Boomer wants options. Ours is no longer a cookie-cutter-funeral society, nor should it be. No two people's lives are the same, so why should anyone have a boilerplate funeral, complete with clergy from a church they don't belong to and a cake-and-cookie reception?

If you want a meaningful and relevant funeral for your mother or father (whether burial or cremation), grab hold of the reins and tell the funeral director this. Funeral directors are not mind readers, they are caretakers. Let them guide you, but be true to your loved one's wishes and speak up!

Funerals don't have to be expensive to be relevant. If finances are limited say so upfront. There is nothing that can't be worked through. It's unfair to expect the funeral home to know what you need and expect unless you are honest.

Baby Boomers have changed the way birth takes place by the use of birthing rooms, knowing the gender of the baby prior to birth, and the way death takes place with the introduction of hospice. Why not come full circle and change funerals too?

This book has been about taking control of your healthcare, your finances, and your or your loved one's end days. If you have gotten this far, you are someone who sees the value in taking control of the inevitable. Preplanning a funeral is a part of that. Doing so allows one to qualify for Medicaid assistance and also gives control over this final act that memorializes your a life and brings closure to loved ones. It is a gift to those who are left behind.

Death, though a sobering experience, can also be bittersweet for the deceased's loved ones; in fact, if handled correctly, it can be a positive experience. You can't stop others from grieving, but by preparing for death (including preplanning and prepaying for a funeral), you can allow your family to concentrate on tending to their emotions. They will be able to share memories and reflect on the happiness their loved one brought to their lives instead of stressing over funeral details or worrying over finances.

FAMILY CARE PLAN

Below are items necessary to complete a death certificate or obituary.

Do not use nicknames or make any assumptions when completing this information since it will be used for the death certificate. Each time a death certificate is changed there is a fee, so it is best to have it completed correctly the first time. All information should match other legal documents such as birth and marriage certificates.

Last Name _____

First Name _____

Maiden Name _____

Middle Initial _____

Date of Birth _____ Birthplace _____

City, State, Country, Zip _____

Social Security Number _____

Legal Residence _____

Address _____

City , State, Zip _____

Married _____

Widowed _____

Single _____

Divorced _____

Spouse's Name _____

Last _____

First _____

Maiden _____

Middle Initial _____

Marriage Date _____ County _____

City and State _____

FAMILY CARE PLAN

Mother's Name _____

First _____

Middle Initial _____

Maiden Name _____

Last Name _____

Father's Name _____

Last _____

First _____

Middle Initial _____

Ancestry of the person arrangements are for (Irish/German, etc.)

_____

Surviving Children: _____

_____

_____

_____

Surviving Grandchildren:

_____

_____

_____

_____

Surviving Siblings: _____

_____

_____

_____

FAMILY CARE PLAN

Proceeded in death by: _____

_____

_____

_____

Type of Service: _____

Burial _____

Cremation _____

Visitation: _____

Same Day _____

Day Prior _____

Both _____

Other _____

Body present: Yes   No

If in a casket, viewed with lid:_____

Open _____

Closed _____

Wood or metal casket? _____

Concrete liner (which does not seal) or sealing vault? _____

What cemetery?

Is there a marker or monument there? _____

If cremated, will cremains be present at the service or memorial gathering?

Yes   No

FAMILY CARE PLAN

Will there be an urn?   Yes   No

Will cremains be buried, scattered, or other? _____

If buried, at what cemetery? _____

Is there a niche, marker, or monument?   Yes   No

Will clergy be present?   Yes   No

Will service take place at a funeral home, a church, or another location? _____

_____

Music? _____

Memorial contributions? _____

Flowers? _____

Photos? _____

Number of death certificates desired: _____
   (These may be necessary to access bank accounts/titles/investments/stocks/bonds, etc.)

FAMILY CARE PLAN

Register of deeds needed?   Yes   No

How will this be paid for: Family   Pre-Paid Insurance   State Assistance   Other

Make sure your funeral home/director:

____ Gives you a general price list for cremation and burial.

____ Asks you for permission to embalm.

____ Will guarantee your contract if qualifying for Medicaid.

____ Will make your contract irrevocable if qualifying for Medicaid.

____ Takes assignment of your funeral contract if qualifying for Medicaid.

____ Verifies that your contract can be transferred to any funeral home of choice. (This may void guaranteed benefits, but all funds are yours.)

____ Explains where your prefunded funeral proceeds are going and provides copies and receipts of all transactions.

____ Obtains the proper authorizing signatures from the family if there is to be cremation.

____ Itemizes costs on the goods-and-services statement:

  _____ Professional services_____

  _____ Merchandise _____

  _____ Cash advance items _____

  _____ State and federal tax _____

  _____ Total _____

Family Care Plan

_____ Asks someone to sign the goods-and-services statement.

_____ Explains payment options.

_____ Offers to file insurance claim(s) on your behalf.

_____ Files for any veterans benefits:
        _____ U.S. flag with a DD214
        _____ Marker or monument unless buried in a U.S. veteran's cemetery
        _____ Military honors (21-gun salute/taps)

Let your funeral director know if the deceased was active in wartime;
there may be benefits available.

_____ Files for any Social Security benefits.
        _____ Spousal one-time benefit ($255)
        _____ Minor children

_____ Completes the obituary in proper format.

_____ Asks someone to proofread all printed materials.

_____ Listens and responds to questions and concerns.

_____ Provides direction for the next steps after the funeral has taken place.

_____ Asks for feedback.

ADDITIONAL RESOURCES

GOVERNMENTAL AGENCIES

Administration on Aging   http://aoa.gov
National Association of Geriatric Care Managers   http://www.caremanager.org
National Center on Elder Abuse (Administration on Aging)   http://www.ncea.aoa.gov
The official U.S. Government for Medicare website   http://www.medicare.gov
The official U.S. Government Medicaid website   http://www.medicaid.gov
The official U.S. Social Security Administration website   http://www.socialsecurity.gov

Senior Care Resource/Products for home health care and seniors   http://www.parentgiving.com

ELDERCARE ABUSE

Nursing Home Abuse   http://www.nursinghomeabuse.net

CARE MANAGEMENT

Aging Help
http//www.Aginghelp.com

For the professional serving the older American through community and in-home services. This help is often identified as senior, aging, or elderly services by organizations that include senior centers, day-care facilities, health clinics, focal point agencies, area agencies, county departments, state units, or other organizations. This site includes job openings, vendor resources, a sharing/assistance area, and planning scanning information. For the latest updates, check out "What's New."

American Academy of Home Health Care Physicians
http://www.aahcp.org

For over a decade, the American Academy of Home Health Care Physicians has served the needs of thousands of physicians and related professionals and agencies interested in improving care of patients in the home. For every elderly person in a nursing home, there are three more people equally fragile and infirm living at home. Home health has become the fastest growing segment of Medicare's budget.

The American Society on Aging (ASA)
http://www.asaging.org

Members comprise of the largest multidisciplinary national community of professionals working with and on behalf of older people. The membership includes representatives of the public and private sectors, service providers, researchers, educators, advocates, health, allied health, social service, managed care and long-term care and mental health professionals, students and the retired, policy makers and planners. For over 40 years, the American Society on Aging has been an active and effective resource for professionals in aging and aging-related fields who want to enhance their ability to promote the well being of aging people and their families.

Aging with dignity
The Five Wishes Booklet

http://www.agingwithdignity.org

ACKNOWLEDGEMENTS

This book is dedicated to my "two Moms." Marie Perkins, both my maternal grandmother and mother are one in the same (she adopted me as an infant), raised me, and encouraged me to set my sights high, to always be true to myself, and to always be a lady.

Janet Switzer was my other mom. I'm not sure who adopted whom, but I'm glad it happened. Janet was also a very wise lady. She reinforced what my mom taught me and also taught me that it is acceptable to be a working mother. She encouraged me to lead by example, which included not putting my life on hold. Janet taught me how to invest, how to save, and when to splurge.

My mom raised me from birth to the age of 23. She died at age 65 of cancer. Janet came into my life a few years later and has been in my life for 23 years. She also died from cancer at the age of 65. I feel so very fortunate that both of my moms have been in my life. I only hope that they learned something from me!